Grendel Liebfraumilch

The rumour that Grendel died on that lonely marsh eight years before proved to be short lived. He was in fact still alive, and kicking against every infuriating obstacle and barrier he could. Waiting for his moment. Planning his atrocities. Working himself up into a frenzy each time he saw a good opportunity pass him by. Occasionally acting on the spur of the moment. The key to his success was of course, the nebulous condition of his occurance. He was quite 'invisible,' except only to the experienced 'ghost-hunter:' undiscovered and free to roam without anyone knowing he was there. But fate can sometimes be very cruel, and as we now know,time was running out. From that undersized room where his gruesome art first made its impression Grendel spread himself across the circuses of the world. Helped by a company pass which didn't cost a penny he boarded several thousand engines and travelled throughout the globe. You only had to defend your creed once to be called a racist in those days.

As he towered above her on the shifting bridge of the ship she cried:

"Grendel, *Grutnachtbist.* Snicker-snacker!"

He shouted back:

"I'm only on the milk round! Why can't you be quiet?"

The result of which she was too scared even to go down to the docks or ask for an ounce of cottage cheese...the devil ran as if there were rocket fuel in his socks. His exorcism became national news and from that moment to this his books were seriously cooked. His arm well and truly torn from it's socket.

For centuries the Golden books of Grendel (or Hel's biscuits) were hidden in a hillside, but were recently brought to light by explorers searching for the source of a strange odour which some campers had reported coming from the river. Many of the sheets were spoiled or covered in a kind of bitchumen oil. A team of volunteers helped to clean them with washing powder and holy water. All sexual behaviour shall be sponged away and must conform to edicts.

FLIGHTS

CANNON,   FABLES,   and the *SUN*

In cap and gown I walked the plank
a blade against my bone,
to leave behind a trail of white,
this legend charred in gold.

Dubloons and trinkets, coins and pearls,
plundered from the banks,
in spirals to the outmost ring,
a mile above the sands.

In legends, flakes, and fine debris,
blown from the edge of stars,
this raincloud from the topmost void,
in gold-dust to the earth.

For legends, fables, and the Sun,
fall scattered on the deck,
these pools of disaffected wine,
spread outward drenched in light.

What *skull* and *crossbones*, torn to shreds,
are hoisted to the mast,
for cannon, rainbows, and the Sun,
are darker than the night.

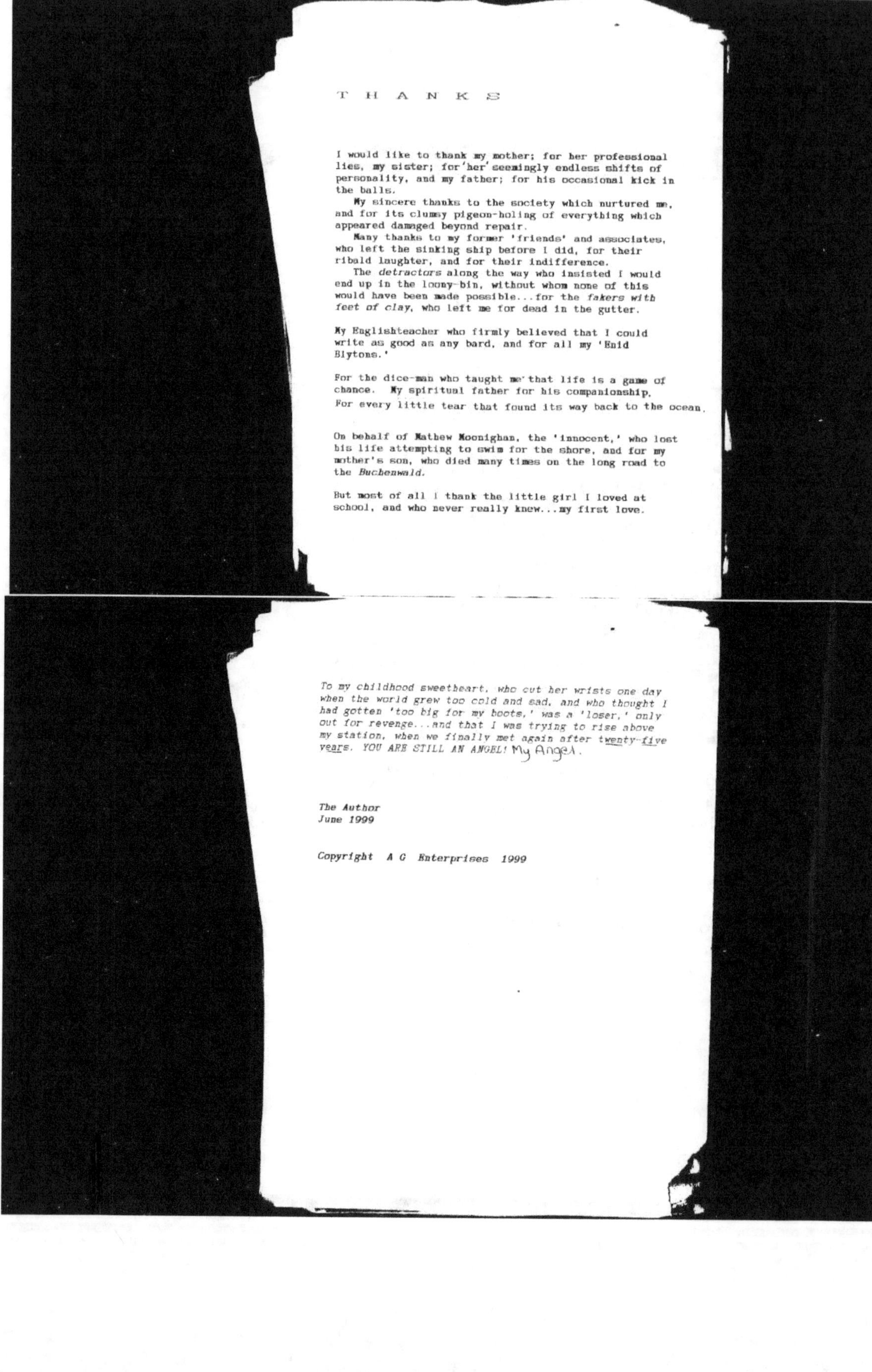

T H A N K S

I would like to thank my mother; for her professional
lies, my sister; for 'her' seemingly endless shifts of
personality, and my father; for his occasional kick in
the balls.
    My sincere thanks to the society which nurtured me,
and for its clumsy pigeon-holing of everything which
appeared damaged beyond repair.
    Many thanks to my former 'friends' and associates,
who left the sinking ship before I did, for their
ribald laughter, and for their indifference.
    The *detractors* along the way who insisted I would
end up in the loony-bin, without whom none of this
would have been made possible...for the *fakers with
feet of clay*, who left me for dead in the gutter.

My Englishteacher who firmly believed that I could
write as good as any bard, and for all my 'Enid
Blytons.'

For the dice-man who taught me that life is a game of
chance. My spiritual father for his companionship.
For every little tear that found its way back to the ocean.

On behalf of Mathew Moonighan, the 'innocent,' who lost
his life attempting to swim for the shore, and for my
mother's son, who died many times on the long road to
the *Buchenwald.*

But most of all I thank the little girl I loved at
school, and who never really knew...my first love.

*To my childhood sweetheart, who cut her wrists one day
when the world grew too cold and sad, and who thought I
had gotten 'too big for my boots,' was a 'loser,' only
out for revenge...and that I was trying to rise above
my station, when we finally met again after twenty-five
years. YOU ARE STILL AN ANGEL!* My Angel.

The Author
June 1999

BILL HYMEN

Where one weird time warp ended another secret
dimension soon sprang into being, with an old alliance
from those days of Yore emerging from her pubescent
chrysalis like a *belle tournure* turned into crow.

It was surprising to discover how just a few short
years since the separation had made such an acute
difference into *impetuous proclivity.*

She squeezed her buxom thighs and slid her hand
coyly across his bump in careful rememberance of the
life of milk and honey, and teased him about his over-
developed rear-guard action. Man-O-Man!

Kylie had been the the most flocculent of her kind,
and somehow at this time, fate had interwoven their
paths once more in pleasant unison.

Had the metamorphosis altered that naturally
harmonious temperament? We shall have to weigh in the
balance how many secrets she could hold.

Kylie Monsoon had always been more flattered by his
perpendicular consideration than her profligate older
brethren, whom she had once unwittingly caught in a
clinch under the bed clothes after a visit to Ramtown.

Her silent bashfulness had made her the misfit, and
in the good old days her mother had chastised her
reluctance to experiment.

The prospect of her daughter dating another male
besides her husband on his less frequent visits to the
dustbin yard filled her with a happy sense of irony.

"What career do you expect to follow now that you've
gained your degree with honours?" she asked.

"Ah!...something unusual I expect," he rambled.
"I'm thinking of applying for entry to the Benedictine
order of vagabonds."

But surely the noiseless foot was way off course?

In a matter of minutes the 'lodger' poked his head in
the door. That was the final straw. After satisfying
himself that the *allies* were up to no good they were
given permission to leave the premises in no uncertain
terms.

"See you all later!" she called..."We're just going
down to flash at the Sisters' of Mercy!" Funny how
word always got around...

When they arrived at the glen the billiard room was
almost in quarantine.

The couple retired to the lounge to discuss the
latest topic of concern over their first social swig as
fully hatched Swallows.

After studying towards her A-levels on Arthur's seat
she hoped to major in Peace studies at a suitable
retreat.

But why did she have to mention the *Arctic seals?*
"I've joined Greenpeace!" she enunciated. Hurrah for
all that! "Don't you care about the rights of
animals?" she snapped. "We must put a stop to this
cruel culling immediately. Scientists are conducting
experiments just so some rich bitch can purchase a
fashionable scent."

She was almost as idiosyncratic as the *'Jellyman'* in
her championing of the underdog. Next thing she would
be migrating to Greenham Common.

Typically, her *outlander* proposed an alternative
solution...an incurable romantic.

"But they'll pay the debt to nature one day anyway,"
he keeked. "We live in an age of 'ocular'
prioritization," said F.

"Why not put their pelts to some good use. Don't
you think that we are all meant to suffer into
knowledge?" he mused; that costly remark certainly
placed the 'cat among the pigeons.'

He reached into his jerkin pocket to pull out the
postcard of that darling pup. Hadn't he fussed around
the hound all afternoon rather than fratinize with the
anthropoids.

But all was not lost, even when she accused him of being an intolerant fascist bastard.

"Let's change the subject," she said. "I don't want to fall out with my childhood idol on our tender reunion date."

"I haven't seen 'Dick' for ages," she reminisced. "I've almost fallen out of the habit. "We *split* three months ago after he returned to the academy..."

When they arrived for the amateur performance of 'the Marriage of Figaro' she seemed apprehensive to approach some of her schoolfriends with such a follically challenged individual.

"I didn't think that you'd have turned out like this," she groaned. "But I suppose you were nearly fully grown when we first met...thankgoodness I remembered to put on my flattest pair of brogues, Dick was over six foot two in inches." Nice one Dick!

A quick peck at the taxi rank as they stood eye to eye did wonders to break the floe of ice. Yet mischief was afoot.

The fully-fledged flashman was perfunctorarily introduced to some of her best bosom chums who scrutinized him closely for further signs of turf.

Here was no stamp straight from Black *Marvel comics*, yet there were still certain traits which matched the hero identically.

In the public house afterwards a joke seemed to be festering in the packed log cabin.

Only the *fat girl* refused to be drawn. Even that quiet space around the corner didn't hide them from the peeps of inquisitive onlookers. With *hoots and pips* the merry band tickled each other with their elbows.

The *fairy boots*, illustrated with an elaborate pattern of animal motifs which mirrored the *Bayeax Tapestry, and* which shone alarmingly over his flame velvet loons... did he not know why the crowd were all grinning?

She was already wearing her *dowdy frump* in order to make him feel less out-of-date.

The *scarlet woman* sat side by side with his bright pink
shirt.

She shyed away from the Seeker to chat at the
opposite end of the table.

Like 'another pair of shoes' the outsider struggled
on, and when he felt she needed to transform her
flagging faith in him he made an effort to impress on
them his *super star status*.

Suddenly one of her friends leaned across and nodded
at his turban...must have been the only person who
didn't have his own *playstation*?

"Are you from Outer-Space?" she gleamed.

Outside the *concentration camp* he offered to give her
free driving lessons...actually it was him who needed
convalescing from post-traumatic stress disorder.

They lay parked in the dark secluded lane smothered
with holly bushes, when he came up for oxygen and
insisted on a chin wag.

"Do you remember that night long ago?" he asked.
"How could I forget," she chuckled. "I've never been
the same since playing whist upstairs. Were there many
in our number?"

The Flash was temporarily caught off balance by this
direct line of questioning...but his senses quickly
recovered and he bounced back with a sting in the tail.

"Oh!...about two hundred or so," he cogitated..."or
enough to form a small legion of honour. But the *lost
tribe* have *foregone the lone islands*...I even loved a
few. For three years I never slept a wink."

"We could always build a *shrine* to them," she
smiled...and began to drink reality.

"My mother says you're still wet behind the collar.
Why don't you drive a harder bargain?"

"You remind me of my dad with your bristly chin,"
she whispered. "It's sexy but I do hope it doesn't give
me a skin rash in the morning."

She stabbed her *longsome wriggler* and locked him in
her iron jaw. With no sense of shame her hand wandered
longingly towards his man-root, until once more she
withdrew as he squealed for a cushion of air.

"Saints alive!" careered the Flash.

His interior felt as if it had been burnished with hot pepper.

But once more he was plunged into the abyss between anxiety and indifference.

Should he simply call it a day now the meat was ooooked?

If he asked her for a fruit gum would she bring him spice? Her mother was putting out *Cooking Fat*.

Beside the nearby runway the engines were shutting down and the *buck-basket* was losing altitude, though she still carried a red flag in her underwear.

"No, not tonight Josaphine," he salvoed, scared stiff the old problemo would rear its fucking head again. Don't let them fool you, or even screw you!

"Perhaps if we could journey back to the future?" Once again the female appeared to have boxed the compass. And just who was the fairest of them all!

"Who said there was going to be a next time!" she smirked...the bird had flown and blown him in a ditch.

BARREN EARTH

"Oyez, Oyez...man on a galloping 'oss wu'nt notis 'em!"
hollered *Cannibal* Joe, as he levelled up the flagging
of the winding spiral staircase for Silcott Planthire.

He squatted down on the ground after kicking the
most salient offender with his size twelve boot, and
eyed the line smartly with his white clay pipe...at
Buckland Villas.

The Foreman returned from doing his star turn and
questioned him thoroughly before the arrival of the
concrete lorry.

"Your dadda's too particlar," he said, lighting up
his furry leaden pipe, and standing back relaxedly.

"Now let's have a cuppa before we make a start. You
worry too much mi young bucko."

Joe removed his brown felt cap and ordered the
driver to mix plenty of lotion in with the mash.

He pointed with the lip of his pipe and scratched
the top of his old grey skull as F. hurried to scatter
the flow, and ordered more fluid from the tap.

The *Oldbuck* had a *flashback* to the nineteen-fifeties
when *time-was* he had first arrived in the dusty *region.*

"Folks were so afraid a me they used to cross to the
other side of the street," he grinned.

Joe had thirty thriving offspring from a dozen
different endearments since those bygone days. And
they said the 'Irish' were taking over the country!

It was impossible for him to memorize all their
names so he simply referred to his male line as
'Sonny.' *Grovel in the dirt and die race of Cain.*

Swore he had more degrees than a thermometer.
Perspiring in the hot summer sun F. dissolved up the
hill after the *tamping* was done and locked the mushroom
door quickly behind him.

At that time in the afternoon Stella would be
situated in the back-bedroom tapping the keys of her
Orion.

The builder in the woolly hat knelt down on the bare
floorboards and waited until she shifted her cursor.

He appeared to be looking out of the bay window and
a callous garden vegetable.

F. attempted to press his features against the
brittleness but his snout hindered further passage that
way.

Since the star was shining so pleasantly in a
spectrum of bright colours she would occasionally
glance in the direction of the newly painted mansion.

Pausing for a moment on her elbow she shielded her
eyes from the direct scorching blaze and wondered who
was flitting at supersonic speed across the southern
hemisphere.

A *soufi* must have caught her attention because
before very long she was holding a large pair of
secoteurs with which to *trim her privet*.

F. paled considerably when he imagined their
possible usage.

Beginning at the far edge of the escarpment she
began to clip the rose bushes nearest the ornamental
statue.

Tampering pedantically around the goldfish pond she
crooned in a world of her own.

There was an interim while her husband paid a visit
from the board of his company.

Frieze had been promoted to prime-shrink among the
persistent cabbages at the house of correction.

Mrs. Do-as-you-would-be-done-by arched stiffly over
the garden gnome with the plump fruits of her buttocks
straining inside her light blue jeans.

Gazing gingerly through the portal he blew his
silver whistle, lurking only inches from the outer
glass where the dove would soon be snipping.

His *dragon breath* heaved noisily toward her wake and
his heart beat like a *paper tyger*.

By the time that *Stella* had arrived in the hollow
recess of the clump the letcherous monster had his
angry erection throbbing hornily in his oily palm.

The *humming bird* knelt on the creaky gravel outside the
nearby square to turn the leaves where the *comet had
landed.*

The woman was more beautiful than he could ever have
dreamt, and they were obviously *sexually compatible...*

In the blessing of *Roentgen*, during the zenith of
summer, she conscientiously fixed her gaping attention
to his glans and willed the creature to reach his
water-shed.

With no regard for his gleam she quaintly
scrutinized the thickness of his peashooter. A fine
projection for the time of year. She concentrated
meanfully on the meandering seasonal flowers along the
circumference.

As the man in the vacant room toiled with increased
vigour she zoomed-in and rooted among the drowsy
glades.

His lobster face seemed fit to explode but he could
not make contact due to the interference of radio
waves. Filled with the ocean's dearest casket.

She stooped soporifically at the eye of the head
like a snow-gnat and reached to wipe the mist away from
the condensed surface, momentarily mislaying her stated
purpose. The earth worms had it!

From the *tulip helmet* a sudden froth of seed erupted
and splattered over the bare wooden panels illuminated
by fire-drake, dropping her clippers. The best of
breeds mingled with the viruses as blur-brain enveloped
the *head gasket* of his hyperthalamus.

Suddenly there was a braying on the panes of the
ventana as he counted his treasures.

Stunned from the yearning he swung round to catch a
glimpse of the tournure as it glided swiftly against
the *curtain of Hyperion*, intimating the veiled presence
of a groundworker disappearing down the landscape
garden, where he had lurked like a 'snake in the
grass...'###!

The chalk of Sam's whirlwind eyes popped menacingly
open as he glared across the factory floor at the fool.

"Stop looking round Kojak or I'm reporting you!" he
felicitated, as the pin-head blonde trotted tartly back
to her sewing machine.

"You were five minutes late this morning!" barked
the Overlooker; pay would be docked accordingly.

Spit the 'wonder' dog, teddy bears, dusty-bins and
Hissing Sid. The whole gamut of cuddly toys were
assembled in preparation for the anniversary rush.

The *skeleton crew* of white galley slaves labouring
on the 'foam-filling spouts' oared clap out to the
hustings. 'Things could only get better!'

For an endless duration the moored alembic
automotons slogged away in the gloom.

"Who loves ya' baby!?" he mocked.
"Lollipop, lollipop," he grinned. The giggling factory
girls aped the cock of the walk.

"Hey Baldy! Why are you so *ugly?*" she screamed.
It was then that F. decided not to enlighten Roxanne,
who he had only recently recognized typing in the
manager's office...

During daylight hours and dormitive epochs the gang
of *dim-wits* wandered down to the works canteen like
pictures from Metropolis for a drink of jungle-juice.

Sambo pushed to the front, and Pinhead hurried so
she could find a place for him next to her.

The alien member of M.E.N.S.A., who had so quickly
been identified rested with the other foam-fillers at
the sparse grubby dinner table.

He was completely conscious of the abrasions neoning
his 'upper storey' like a blurred vision of Jupiter and
the craters of Luna...it was uncanny how cleverly the
illiterate mob were able to manipulate their
instinctive telescopes.

"I I b-b-e-t, I b-b-e-t, I b-b-e-t he'd think t-
twice," whined Stanley the 'Stammerer.' It was no use
'passing the buck' he said. Desperate to keep his
boots clean in a muddy field.

He turned his head towards 'Queenie' complaining
vigorously about the earthdevil.

The *potato head* obliterated with *thrush* saw him reach
self consciously for his cup of honest charr...

"My God, is something wrong with his neck?" she
uttered queerly as he lit..."You turned round then as
if your whole neck was made of *Clockwork!*" she astutely
chimed.

The lumpers burst into rhyme. He reached for the
sky.

The overwrought woman with oleaginous red cheeks
loitered before the *odd-fish* hoping to make him a
complete laughing-stock.

"Come on *Bald Eagle!*" she called out crudely in her
regimented smock. "It's time to get back to the
grindstone."

For once F. managed to hold her attention and did
not look apologetically away, or slowly down to his
chest...

"Er! What's that lump on your face?" he asked
curiously as the middle-aged nag came to a sudden
standstill.

Queenie anxiously examined her crust, feeling over
the grain where the *suet dumpling* excesses seasoned
from late-night drenching. Said she felt as right as
rain.

"Where?" she snapped. She suddenly became a blade
in the wind. "Lump, what lump?" Self-indulgence.

"Ooops! I'm terribly sorry," he rescinded..."It's
your nose that I was looking at!"

With the world at his feet. 'There' was an
earthquake. The earth moved. How was it for you?

She tottered resiliently and flushed. Queenie tried
to regain her composure, but eventually left the room.

The *inverted uterus* pulsed like a *seismic
disturbance*. Study the room temperature.

They slowly returned down the dusthole.
Mounted on F.'s stool was a small brown parcel. He
untied the string. At least they had spelt his
pseudonym correctly.

Eyes stole down to the *isthmus* as he altered his field
of vision... what could it be? Had his reputation
soared during mealbreak? Two for the price of one!
    Out dropped a white bar of *soap* and landed on the
swab deck...

It was difficult to unearth just where *Shittlegruber*
had materialized from. Some of the mutants said that
he was a Pole who had been a prisoner of war and had
fled the Nazi concentration camps, others that he was
in all probability a cryptic German commandant who only
pretended to be semi-illiterate.

Certainly his tales about scoffing six whole loafs
of bread in quick succession while tramping the
indigent *Alsatian den* of Soho, where he met his future
wife in 1945, appeared all Lombard street to a China
orange.

In actual fact he was neither of these.
Shittlegruber was an extra-terrestrial who had
teleported from a *waste disposal vessel* on the planet
Smorg!

It was on the first day of April that the head of
Outdoor machinery had first taken him along to be
introduced to the *lampman* in the bowels of the
suppurated planet.

They abandoned the main depot to march a hundred
paces across the hinterland of fag-end droppings.
Along the black diamond banks of nutty slack the hovels
of burnt-out brake-vans littered the derelict landscape
like a division of sundry spooks.

Then the search party emerged into the huge
neolithic hall of the slatternly cargo bay long since
superceded.

The *Marksman* opened the old wooden door in the
ground which led down to the ancient railway catacombs
beneath the *Terminus's* long and bleak irregular
platforms.

Trammelling the deep-toned Fallopian tube to
stronger smells of urine their fading shadows arrived
at a dark little room at the end of the dim Victorian
tunnel...a shabby creature stirred in the squalid light

upon what appeared to be a recently planted dunghill.

Perched in the shabby rat-pit connected by cobbles to the bunker of the Town's Wool Exchange, and with the noisy rattle of the sewer stream pervading through an even darker corner of the cell, the *lampman* anxiously palpitated at the acoustic approach of invidious intruders. He sliced his raisin in half!

He hostled the endemic plastic beaker with a grubby pewter spoon which looked as if it had been dipped in the raff down below...he was reputed to fret his hours on grouts and packets of Seabrooke.

Bulbs of every description littered the walls and shelves in the murky cave of the 'Lighthouse.' With a flourish of dreary trumpets a cathedral of immigrant castes threw shilly-shally on the wall like a spray of *Aniline dyes*.

The old Troglodyte in his tatty Proletarian dudes buttressed against the red brick like a small brown bear rubbing his dull grey eyes. An awry coat-hanger fixed his distempered snotrags steaming over the fireplace. He shuffled in his sludge mumbling sour anathemas. The overclouded lantern swinging on the brad concerned his swarthy snout with an aspect of vague perplexity as he crabbed to peer beyond the ghosts of pliant cobwebs.

Uncertain light from the dusty P. way oil lamp fluxed in a warm nebulous breeze which originated from the invisible welkin satellite, and a morose yellow colour trickled with the moisture sliding down the decaying archaic timber.

The anchoretic Lampman offered his mawler in a vale of sorrows towards the impure 'time-traveller' with a *standard of Herpes* underscored on his spur.

"I want you to teach him the *cresset* throughout the entire *Great Western network*. We expect you both to work in regular harmony."

Strange prehistoric sounds juddered in the scurvy gullet of the lampman. The swollen tongue protested vehemently for not even a sigh and his acrobatic tonsils could be seen doing somersaults on the stage of his deleterious chamber. Increscunt animi!

His primeval birdlike eyes glittered beneath the
gleaming fictile wing of his 19th century helmet and
began to jump overboard.

F. listened impassively as the cringing *creole*
descended into a hotbed of fevered and fustian
gibberish. The only probable quiddity that prospered
around *Shittlegruber* was the sybaritic *family of warts*
perched in the right sided crevasse of his massive
snout. They pointed like a graph of adherent
skyscrapers in the direction of the *Gate of Mars* and
gave his 'crocadile hide' a lopsided pitch.

Greenwood produced a piece of floppy litmus from his
upper pocket which flickered luminously in the sub-
lunar closet and which threatened to blow away in a
sudden gust...Was some shadey contract being signed?
Who were the guilty parties involved?

With Shittlegruber's *feather quill* F. copied the
line of words and spelled his own name correctly on the
target. Amazing window of opportunity.

The lucubrate studiously examined his efforts, as
the eremite sunk sharply back into shadows, pretending
to tidy up the maculated shit-tip at his desk.
Greenwood seemed rather pleased that he had been able
to copy the work correctly, and unlike his quaint
companion would not simply have to place an X to
receive his weekly *greenbacks!*

The sorry Lampman ushered them sulkily to the
entrance through the low Caspian arch in an attitude of
beggary with the *dandruff infested billy-cock* grasped
tightly in his pap.

'Alice' had no time to play on the swings like the
other girls' he bewailed.

As the *Senior electrician* turned to wish him fond
farewell at the warren mouth the *Lampman* whimpered
gratefully, and bowed graciously in a supreme
expression of absolute penury.

"Don't worry Boris," sibilated the 'Overman.'
"Now you'll have a regular partner who can fill in
those crucial time-sheets (His eyes achieved a misty
look)." Once had an electric cable fall on him.

Shittlegruber aimed a spag at the cockroach which had
crept hesitantly from the shallow winter's grill over
the ruddy channel. Under normal circumstances he would
have crunched the horn and roasted it on a spit.
     He waited until the creature balanced on the lip of
his lunch box before toppling the insect with a liberal
helping of gum. The old Lampman gave a joyous cry and
cackled..."Bullseye!" Stacks of compensation.
     As they abandoned the *reeking grotto* to stoop once
more along the nigrescent route beneath the law courts
the apprentice could not help hearing Greenwood mutter
under tone. They stumbled towards the dank
subterannean gallery where it was possible for the
lanky Supervisor to stand. He turned to shout.
     "Aren't you going to do any work today you fat
Polish bastard!" he boomed down the honeycomb.

'Keeper of light let me look and see, the pattern of
your life shine on your tapestry?' There was rumoured
to be a purge by the *jarvey* on any *deadwood* in the
vicinity...Previous experience? Lavatory attendant.
     Along the platform the old man struggled to drag the
heavy cylinder spring, with F. prancing on ahead and
hoping not to meet anyone he knew.
     The pockets of his long dark greatcoat were crammed
like sardines with *Halogen* lamps as he urged him to
have a little consideration for flinching steps.
     Old Shittlegruber plodded against the hive stream of
rushhour bees hid below the black rim of his helmet
like a petrified ancient mariner. Pushed against the
subway wall the *Lampman* reached for his trusty
screwdriver whose broken handle was a testament to his
fortitude, and forty years of slapping salami in the
service.
     F. climbed the battle-worn fort scaffolding, whose
creaking ebon structure, flaking with autumn colours,
resembled the horse built for the storming of barbican,
and which was normally chained inside a perimeter of
tungsten at a tangent to the traffic.

More preoccupied by the passing talent, and full of wish-fulfillment towards the possibilities unfolding, he broke the cellotape surrounding the old cardboard home. The lampman recovered the phosphorescent bulb with his faces glowing...a replacement for the *Argand* long ago found faulty.

F. carefully fitted the article into the gap vacated by the old cartridge which had blown.

Before tackling the turret on the station flats they payed a visit into the booking office, where the backroom staff were busy swilling amphetamines.

As F. climbed the doubtful aid a burst of laughter fired from their jaws. Shittlegruber's pins were literally covered in *varicose veins.*

When the *magician's apprentice* had reached the top of the ladder, clinging delicately to the 'conjuror's rope,' and had opened the fitment ready for purging, his mate down below started to rinse out that old woollen rag...

Mangling the raiment in the leaky tin pail Shittlegruber reached up to his associate and tried to hand him the material as if it were a fine piece of bone china, while trying to hold the platform steady with his other trembling pad.

It hit Shittzel-gruber directly on the neck where his rash of rancid boils were erupting like never before.

The old man exploded like a bomb shell! "P-e-e-zzda!" he roared in his strong gutter-all accent, and the dim grey eyes clouded dully over, as he attempted to remove the stain from his dirty ramshackle hod.

His attempt at retaliation landed in the travel clerks mug...

Once more Shittlegruber reached reluctantly for the firmament with his pudding thumb quaking like a reluctant crane, and clutching the chipped resin handle of the screwing implement above his rotting mildewed eyes.

The new recruit scratched his head and reckoned to
reach down but couldn't quite make a connection. A
wedding party gaped through the booking office parlour.

His glazed red eyes became gradually more dense as
the Flasher stared into the enormous black shafts which
were his nostrils. The short swarthy Shittlegruber
stammered, with the sides of his huge beak flapping
like a pincered bat.

"Oh! C-C-come on," he complained bitterly. "We have
the station concourse to do after this and it's nearly
tiffin already."

The zoot-suiters poleaxed along to the next case
outside the dock as the Wedding party blithely
scattered confetti over the happy couple, slamming the
door in haste.

O'Flanagan leered from the solitary ticket barrier.
Once more old grey hair passed up the sponge from the
cold bucket of bilge-water for the cover cleaning.

From a considerable height F. squeezed the juicy oil
cloth causing a trickle of the stinging fluid to drip
straight into the corner of Shittlegruber's *rufous
dish*. While his partner was cursing the material
slipped from his hand and saddled over one of the
instructor's funnel ears.

The railway cap fell awkwardly to his shoulder and
hung on his back, while the EASTERN EUROPEAN seemed to
lose his balance in an effort to prevent the
embarrassing calamity.

Shittlegruber raked obstreperously at the endless
tract of straggle in an effort to disguise his
macerated *chrome-dome*.

The lampman's crass dilated holes suggested a
complete lack of cranial activity. No matter how much
he was put to the question the lampman would never look
F. directly in the eye, but would stare blankly at the
side wall or exit. No-body could be that stupid could
they...could they?

In tragic farce he chased desperately down the
platform followed by a strong gust of wind among the

packed voyagers, clutching his parrot's peak with one
hand, and reaching periodically for his tourniquet with
the other...

Shittlegruber carefully unpacked his carrier of
tricks, and laid the priceless rag over the hanger.

"You might as well bugger off now," he insisted,
'but I'll hang on a few ticks just in case Greenwood
checks up.'

Feigning to leave the shell of the hermitage F.
sneaked surreptitiously back around the portal, only to
find Shittlegruber tirelessly ploughing his shreds with
his head between his legs.

The Lampman meticulously arranging his *idiosyncratic*
threads like a scrupulous flower arranger, muttering
foul obscenities, dashed instinctively for his pair of
pliers.

"You're not a bad twat really," he growled in his
strong guttural drawl. "For a cunt that is!" His
watering eyes twinkled with assinine sadness.

The horrible black-pitted skin grew more mucoused as
his fingernails continued chaffing. A poxy rash which
spread from his etiolate body now threatened to consume
even the tarred complexion.

With a vindictive stare Shittlegruber finished
toying with his stack, and with a malevolent grin of
equal joy spoke brashly to his *novus homo.*

He rekindled his railway helmet intact, shuffling
the ends of straw inside the filthy up-turned collar of
his stump.

"I'm gaining on sixety," he grimaced in his drawling
burr, "but I've got more hair than you'll ever
have"...then he guffawed like a squealyy mule.

"I know what's wrong with you!" he snapped..."You're
just not getting enough *shark liver.*"

Even in the depths of the hottest summer the aged
lampman refused to remove his long greatcoat, or
surrender his *Arsenal scarf.* His English seemed
retarded to say the least and the verbiage of his

national tongue was even harder to solicit. Surely this was taking the guano??

As the two stooges boarded the train to *Buckfast Abbey* F.'s tongue was almost dragging along the platform kerb.

They sat side by side to start with...then F. began to play his game of 'musical chairs,' preferably in a 'non-smoking compartment.'

'Look mum, it's the 'Minder!' shouted a little boy as he hurried on the steeplechase.

Much to his annoyance *Shittlegruber* swetted in his wake.

What a piece of luck, the cat had really landed on its feet! He kicked the sand in his ugly mug.

F. quickly found a seat near the respectable professional *Civil Servant* browsing a copy of Cosmopolitan, but the lampman's enormous beak still peered over the top of the seat a couple of spaces behind.

How would he dare to pilot the unthinkable in so glaring a fashion? The temptation to do something dreadful burnt like a *forest fire* in his loaf. Shock horror probe!

Shittlegruber slyly lit a tab and feigned to keep good faith with the lunar landscape, his beady eyes flashing immediately away whenever F. caught him surreptitiously stealing a glance.

Stage by perverted stage the rotter gradually released his straining lightning conductor beneath the obscure auspices of his black-leather Bomber jacket.

With only his step-ins to go the lampman seemed in the land of Nod.

The nice piece of skirt cleared her smooth white throat and edged a little closer to the exit. With avid curiosity she switched on her livid concentration as the fiendish drama unfolded. A tight knot twisted in his stomach as he candidly exposed his jury-pole. The pimpled conductor had the audacity to pester them for their *identity cards*, with a tantalizing display of tension, arresting his development.

In a moment of *divine inspiration* he succeeded in
holding the ring around his iron lantern, and mocked
her ghoulish interest with a multitude of rhythms. Her
ecstatic eyes fogged with snow as the pervert's
erection grew. Like a gnarled rod the impoverished
penis faintly smiled and made her shiver.

A feeling of complete nausia bourned like simmering
midnight as he sickly contemplated reaching *rocket
launch*. He vowed that on the next occasion he would
not wear any such encumberances.

The sight of her goose-pimpled thighs made his heart
race faster. She had matured considerably since the
Grammar School where she had been captain of that
winning netball team.

The lids of the surprised *sightseer* opened and
closed like a pair of drafty shutters as he initiated a
further late edition of his *daring auxiliary
supplement*.

Her heaving boobs drooped over the couch exposing
her brassiere line near the deserted moss of the Peace
Hall.

With each new fifth her face grew increasingly
cadmium. *The favourite's* concern managed to manifest
itself on the gleaming glans with obvious guilty
feelings and ambition.

Should he or shouldn't he if that was what she
really desired? Bring herself to climax...bring
himself to climax? - In a public place? Why, that's
indecent!

Her dreamy eyes lustfully melted over and an
uncontrolled dribble of saliva trickled from her gum
shield, as she deliberately placed her magazine on the
rack so that she could suck his brains without anymore
bothersome distractions.

There was a lingering doubt that something could be
out-of-step though.

The sand of the egg-timer shuttered towards a
showdown. The destination station quickly approached
on the horizon, as the *figure-head* hummed intensely to
his loathsome mesmeric tune.

With the train juddering to a sudden stand he suddenly
found his pneumatic drill beginning to ejaculate into
the sleeve of his jacket. Out of the corner of his eye
he noticed Shittelgruber wide-awake and chuckling
furtively. *Tarred and feathered* the mutant sneered to
the top of his bent.

The old cardboard box stationed upon his knee
rattled with its *Noah's Ark* of moons...F. was ready to
make a disconcerted rush for the door but already there
were frowns.

Greasy globs of soup poured down the Lampman's
apelike brow as he stared succinctly forward making a
loud clicking noise in his throat.

As F. wiped away the semen with his cuff the
Chartered Accountant reading his *Daily Star* gaped with
shock and horror as if he'd just caught a chiller.

With her eyes tied to the spot she dangled at his
heels down the crowded rostrum. Her pegs loitered
longingly around his loins, and scrutinized his
muscular frame and tiny midrift.

Her face appeared to be made of marble. She seemed
on the verge of a *mental breakdown. He paced quickly
ahead of the charging Nimrod.*

Then he saw Shittlegruber pop up round the corner
like a startled Jack-rabbit. He emerged from the hat
of the darkened waiting room.'Rollercoaster.'

·Without a single shred of remorse the *space-man*
grinned and carried on his craft. The old fellow
turned devoid of any care.

"Had to leave you!" trajected Shittlegruber in a
crisp sycophantic jarlance..."see man about dog."

The Flashman manoevered nervously in his chancery
suit.

Out in the yard of *Barmy street* in those days appeared
the weird and wonderful sight of a mongrel horde
teleported from some distant universe and dropped in
the ocean of humanity.

It was as if a giant collector had scoured the

unknown void for specimens to populate the large
expanse of barren land at the run-down 'Carriage and
Wagon' depot.
        The *Moloch* had spitefully dumped them all in the
centre of this iron-bridge paddock.
        When the Ordinance Survey were conducting one of
their shoots the entire scene had to be photographed
again because an inmate at this bizarre location had
accidentally lifted a finger...
        Visitors from another world often brought a wry
smile to the corners of his mouth, although words of
native *gen* were never answered by anything but a
sinister grin from the timekeeper.
        In return for a small bonus he could be viewed
menstruating in his space suit, after completing an 'F'
clean, from the underside of the Snake's oily belly.
        With a hand that had never heard of manicure he
rubbed his increasing chalk circle, and trundled
forward like a 'Mary Shelley $ doll.'
        Evolving blotches marked the bald indentations of
his skin with what appeared to be pigeon droppings from
his drill around the Town Hall Chamber every sunrise.
What survived of his dentures were laced with crape.
His pincers were weathered with a leprosy of nicotine.
        "When ya getting married then?" tiraded the fitters
as they passed into the shop. You worthless piece of ....
        The *living corpse* began to rave at the top of his
voice and pulled on his pointed beard. His mits were
fastened to the handle of the swabber along the lanes.
        Eagleburger had been in and out of the loony-bin
ever since his first barney in the Glasshouse. He
always returned in a deeper state of trauma. His arms
seemed alive with shingles as he discovered his hoary
whiskers and became etched to the spot.
        "Whaaa..! Whaaa..ya doing?" he would plagiarize
them, as they quizzed him about which day it
was....that had him foxed for quite a while!
        "Whaa! Whaa...ya doing?" he nagged in his winsome
wailing timbre, scrubbing his pot belly and scratching
in his arse-crease.

They logged their presence and asked for permission to
enter the channels of the underground lighting far
below the sunroof.

The odd couple of dregs negotiated their path to the
dark recesses of yonder shed, where the Pit lights were
always covered in excrement from the rolling stock
above.

As they squelched around in the foul muddy waters
only Shittlegruber seemed at home in the stinking
environment.

He would reminisce sentimentally about the past as
he splashed along the quagmire. He buzzed beside the
frosted glass suddenly brimmed with youthful vigour.

"You should have been on the bandwagon in 1949!" he
hissed. Gagging for a fuck!

Apparently they were all oil lamps in those days.
His link-boys had to climb the fuselage up the
signalling poles to explain the *Sphagetti Junction*
beneath them. Brundled with self-esteem!

He retold the cautionary tale about one of his
greatest exploits...A partnership made in heaven!

After exchanging crockery across the room he had
chased his naked spouse into the cellar of their
neighbours house which adjoined onto theirs, where the
wife was flogging the ironing, with an erection in one
hand and a Carving knife in the other.

"A goodman!" gasped the Judge. "So why are you
emigrating?" The half-crazy Lamper.

Shittlegruber's merry eyes glittered warmly in the
safety of the hot obtenebration as he fiddled with the
rods that locked the casing and prevented their clear
exposure.Darker than a black Jew's stinkpot.

As he opened the panelling like a box of 'Turkish
delight' the glow of the streamer coruscated his
creeping psoriasis. In the choking vicinity of the
exhaust fumes his tool fell from his grip only to be
submerged in the bogslime.

There were a thousand *stained glass windows* to be
holystoned before attending to their gastronomic
requirements.

The old Lampman's bottomless black wells cradled
upwards towards the latrine rim of the silver wheel,
and called for another implement to be borrowed from
the nearby mob.

"Go see if they have a spare..." he begged.
The door was ajar to their open cess pool so he
cautiously entered the Den-of-*lazy-bones*.

Dregs and dottle were scattered around the huge oak
benches of their cabin hartalling their gambolling
caper.

A stale stench from the *Fatman's* obese hull fouled
the rancid air with its reeking perfume as he traipsed
across the clinkered ground of their 'fleapit.'

The sudden activity caused some of the workers to
stir their heavy eyelids and fribble from their cat-
nap. This hut of ill repute could certainly have done
with a squirt from that well known brand of *cleaning
fluid*! The waters of *Lethe*.

A hazy cloud of smoke rose up from Alec's pipe and
obstructed the passage of light as Flash stumbled like
the *waiter on Providence.*

With his 'parker' pulled tight over his head, and a
boyish bloom upon his weary face, he hesitated on the
border of the orlop deck.

A host of malodorous men omniverously callipered his
form as he stammered for a spare 'screwdriver.' He
could feel the eyes of *Ludlam's beast* eating into his
flesh with a copulatory gaze.

Suddenly their Crow-haired-young-ganger emerged from
the greasy secluded kitchen where he had been hawking
the stranger, as he wavered self-consciously in the
hornet of the smoking-room. A flame still burnt upon
the filthy nigger stove.

At first glance F. did not twig the waggery.
"I've only got the one!" smirked *Tarbuck* facetiously,
as he tossed his semi-erect penis... "but it's a wee
bit blunt I'm afraid."

From the open grassland Flashman chased the Lampman
into the soot secluded cloisters, brandishing the

nettle reed before him, and trying to sting the old
man's hand held defensively at his rear.

Eventually they terminated in the drab and dreary
works canteen where Shittlegruber attempted to
hibernate until hang up.

As he slouched into a half-baked kip he was suddenly
awoken by a teabag as it splattered against his
lughole. The ruptured contents mingled with the harsh
red boils festering on the flange of his withered
collar.

It was almost time for the crafty shark to go on
extended shore-leave.

Shittlegruber spat like a cornered alley-cat. His
stunted neck twitched in a final death-throw as he
pleaded for an end to hostilities.

When the Shop-office-man appeared on the scene he
seemed like a fish-out-of-water.

Starbuck appeared intent on bearing a grudge over
the omission of certain items in his case history.

His words were flung from a frozen glacier.
"Don't you think you should have told them?" he
insisted.

"What if they should discover your unfavourable
verdict by another route?"

The old fellow was snoring loudly in the cockshut
time...

"Alright! Where's 'Gunga Dinn?'" he sneered.
sarcastically. "We have a warrant for his arrest" he
joked....There was something about a ladder hidden in
the grass.

"H-h-he's up on the roof sunbathing!" responded
Shittlegruber; that was the third time he'd been
reported in only one week for tanning his organ.

Why orgasm at the end of the street when a free pass
meant unheralded freedom up and down the countryside?

Before long F. was on his way to an interview at
Rail Lodge.

In a land of loaves and fishes he might be offered a
post as *Captain* of the 'Traveller's Fare.'

A brand new pullover just fitted the bill as he boarded
the intercity Pullman locomotive with high hopes of
gaining the upper hand.

There is no need to exaggerate his electrification
when an attractive auburn-haired executive embarking on
her journey at Sherwood specifically chose a seat right
beside the squarepusher.

The lady retrieved her business documents from the
padlocked briefcase, and began to concentrate on her
confection.

F. slowly extorted his sermon after only half a
minutes seedy deliberation toward the promised land.

By operating his voodoo on the gawking window-
shopper F. was able to succumb his restrictive manacle.

Throughout the march of spring she organized her
Gladstone, sliding the catch which afforded an adequate
shield from their prying *hall of audience*, adjusting
her bra strap and preening her adequate shoulder
padding. To cut a long story short···

Eventually she reached for her cosmetic bag,
resolving to unclip her pink Oyster shell mirror,
pouting her admirable lips with *mauve paint*, and
colouring with a touch of *actor's rouge* around the
optical basilisk.

It was during her mascara phase that he suddenly
noticed her correct disposition eyeballing him, where
the light shone directly between his meridian haze.
She gravitated towards his *angry taper* where the chasm
erupted along the fault line; inviting her to dine.

His penis eye peeped gingerly out from the row of
tanned buttons like the blind lid of a Cyclops, filling
with the hydraulics of consanguineous intentions.

The pillar of concrete with its magnificent neon-
tube flushed like a beacon to all who were in agony of
its presence. The innocent lamp.

"Excuse me please!" She leaned across to deck the
Dunhill in the ashtray which they shared in collusion.

Whiffling his wispy filament the flustered Flasher
spurted his excess fare high into the luggage rack as
the ship veered to starboard.

Thirteen spurts and no 'passes'..."Just like
that!"...thank you very much sir!

"Thankyou," she said..."thankyou very much!" she
glimmed, winking genially enough to rouse the cockles
of his gross infatuation.

But the best laid schemes of mice and men had been
known to go astray.

The *tax inspector* turned over her files to begin
anew.

It was then that the Fabulous Flash noticed the
hideous blain which tarnished the front of his brand-
new livery.

He had completed his wayfaring both *'outward'* and
'return' for the ump'teenth time later that afternoon
when he became aware of a reception committee standing
by on the station forecourt.

As he dismounted among the other palmers he
endeavoured to ignore the belligerant coastguard
crouched at the turnkey. Take a dive!

Attempting to appear incognito he deviated towards
the *fire escape* which led to his Batmobile.

Shittlegruber earmarked the oddity with the inspired
chuff of a Judas goat at the parting of the waves.

Mike Winter tipped his snitch as F. wriggled like a
cat at Crufts. Head of the Mafia.

"That's the little prat!" he barked. "He's the egghead spotted travelling up and down the branchline
without any reasonable excuse.".

At the *iron gate* 'Winter' collared him, and read the
Wanderer rights. They led F. into the office for an
immediate interrogation. He had it bloody coming!

With the bright overhead spotlight radiating in his
crystalline lens they demanded to know what he had been
doing sight-seeing on the *bug-train*. He WAS sitting in it!

"Harry Ramsdens?" he scoffed. "Your duty pass only
permits restricted travel. Let me have a look!"

"So you were visiting the 'Lighthouse' for spare
safety-lamps?" taunted the detective.

"Let me just ask Mr. Shitt-eel-gruber to confirm your
unlikely story. Until then you'll be detained for
further detailed questioning."
     That awful word 'redundancy' had been muttered.
Words like 'the sack,' lay-off/turn-off, give the boot,
given the push, order off, take one's wicket, exorcize!
     The episode confirmed that F. had just lost one of
his nine 'feline' lives!

OH, WELL!

"Either 'he' goes or 'I' go!" raved the lodger at the
top of his voice..."What he needs is a brain transplant
not a hair transplant! I'm not putting up with that
funny bastard a second more. I had a different bird
every night at his age," he boasted.

The *practical family man* was living proof of the
cliche that behind every successful entrepreneur *lies* a
'good woman;' he had just packed his job in once more
because the firm were 'doing it all wrong again!' With
a finger in every pie he showered the woman with
trinkets. A pile of moth-balled scrap still lodged
against the scallop. Cannibal Joe had rang to say he
would be 'on the job all day.' The bleeder chuckled.

She lolled dreamily on the 'Bodger's' shoulder
maudling simpering noises of gratitude and fussing
round his loin cloth. When she cottoned-on to the
outside edge she repeated the act with added relish.
And of course the Bodger never looked at any other
woman. She seemed determined to prove that he was not
naturally aggressive; but led astray by his peers.

She called F. a buffoon, but it only sounded like a
typical piece of myth building. He 'hadn't got the
brains he was born with.' So he was told...gobll-

There must have been some way in which F. formed the
syllables in his mouth that provoked an immediate
antagonistic response as he swayed in the *high wind* of
the flight path. Mixed with the wrong crowd all day!

"I just want to have a good time!" she insisted,
grossly simulating the sounds of her animal orgasm.

"You spoil everything," she sneered. She snickered
at his complete impuissance, happy as a Sand girl. "I
won't have any foul language in my house."

"I don't mind admitting that you are a real
disappointment to me," she sighed. "Even your puerile
little father wasn't so peculiar. You beggar all
description."

"Let's examine my new *bidet*," exuded the schoolteacher
while salivating 'babytalk.' "He couldn't knock the
skin off a rice pudding."

"If you can find them you can have them!" she
hissed, as he scampered round the roseberry bush trying
to catch his dirty linen.

"I'll never forgive the way you've behaved!" she
vowed sacriligiously.

"After all we've done to help you. I've always been
a very homely person myself but you've outstayed your
welcome!"

"But why did you have to slash down the Oak?" he
asked. Here was a wretched trimming they could easily
afford to shed.

"Mind your own fucking business and 'Piss off!'"
snapped the 'Bodger.'

The little woman held him back with her mit, and
curtailed her lecture from the lectern of the stepfoot
dais, before he earnestly departed down the road. By
hook or by crook she would leach her itching palm.

"You've got no right to criticize anyone the way you
carry on!" mocked the hag. "I've had a rotten life
because of you. Just sling your flipping hook."

"If you're still hanging around at sundown Bobby
will be across to turf you out of the yard. I've never
forgotten the way that you split up our family by your
performance."

"I take it you want me to leave then?" he enquired.
The underdog tinkered with the plastic bags containing
his belongings, and dusted the *dross* from some of his
underclothes. More sleepless nights than a jumping bean!

"I can defend 'my' pulling of oars with the right of
primary premise," he stammered.

The thought occurred for him to mention the fact
that Jellybates was in fact three years his senior, and
he still lived at home with his mother, but he didn't
want to provoke her further because he'd noticed the
absence of his toothbrush.

"You forgot to pack my toothbrush?" he parsed.
"Don't you worry about that!" she snapped. "We'll post
it to you in an envelope! Ring the 'Secret Society' if
you've got a problem. Take it somewhere else but don't
bother us because we're too busy. Nature never
intended you to be so big," she hissed. "You'll never
shift sand while you still have a hole in your arse."

She held the phone in her hand and begged them to
send a *removal van* to evict him. The volunteer agreed
that it was high time for him to go..."Good riddance to
bad rubbish!" Not much to look at either.

Persuaded by his pretty wife to show pity on the
'throw-out' Ryan Starbuck reluctantly agreed to let him
lodge in the cold stark *Attic*, so long as he paid his
dues every payday.

That first evening in the cabin she seemed glad to
have someone to reciprocate with. The experienced
dental nurse made them all a chota hazri. They sat at
the supper table and ruminated.

For an hour he'd lurked pensively in the darkness
outside their establishment, considering whether to
masturbate so close beside the Superintendent's
palatial residence, with her silhouette jamming at the
keyboard.

"Hurry up wife!" ordered the 'Big man' as she
laboured tiredly at the ring.

It was two years since they had been married at the
Catholic church on *Buckfast road* and both their feet
were getting slightly fidgety.

The 'property' offered F. the *Cream* she had been
saving. It was her intention that they should sign him
into the health club on their 'family membership.'

'He' avoided announcing his *life ban* for peeping
into the ladies' sprinkler. That horrid memory
triggered *specters* of the unfortunate incident when the
owner had listed the number of complaints before his
staff counter.

F. unpacked 'Clippy-the-Great' his self-shearing
combine.

"I never liked the look of Buster Bloodvessel," he
impugned...

Ryan Starbuck admonished her active dispensation.
"Why are you wearing that low cut dress tonight?" he
baulked.

His 'sperm count' had been well above average, so
why had he been unable to father any offspring?

It had been the very same that afternoon at the 'tug
of war' on the Church Green where F. had acted as their
Anchor man.

Instead of shouting for her husband as you might
have expected Abigail had chosen to scream for *him*,
until her chords had snapped.

How could one concentrate with that racket going on
behind him.

"I've heard all about you!" smiled her mother.
"Abigail never talks about anyone else..."

Then the Blonde Bombshell placed his hand on her
right leg to feel her knee joint click. The rest of
the mob had stared aghast at an act which would surely
have resulted in their limb being uprooted from its
socket...

"You're not like the rest of his chums I have to
say. Most of them are arrogant and conceited. Do you
still write to our friend Erna in the Netherlands?
That was a pleasant young man I saw you with. He
seemed gentle and sensitive like you. Where did you
meet him, at college?!"

"When you do find the right girl I'm sure that she
will need to be very special indeed. Shall I make you
a date with Judith? She's got a nose just like *Concorde*
too!"

"Don't get the wrong idea, she doesn't fancy you or
anything, but she finds you an extremely good gagster,
and says that you are an awfully nice chap, although
'you'd' probably get bored with her before much time
had elapsed."

"She might be a lot happier with you than with the
geyser who knocked her all over the place."

"Why don't you try it?" she teased. "You might even enjoy it! Don't tell Ryan, but I've just had another miscarriage. I'm not ruining my figure just to please him. He says that you have a *Persecution complex*...You're the only person I know who irons his own underpants."

In the newly painted living room the Minor bird had ejected its droppings like a demented J.C.B. She was said to prefer a cock-or-two. But Ryan threatened that if he ever caught her...more work on the peck-deck.

Although their home was not studded with sparklers Abigail lived in hope and admitted that at least her husband could not have been any more handsome.

Julian arrived down from the bedroom, and flew into the kitchen when he heard that *the hound from hell* was up from the *bottomlands*.

Tyson had been bolting down his diet of 'sheep's stomachs,' which he regurgitated in his haste, and immediately gobbled down again...

Those teasing taps on the van window at Barmy street had turned the foaming bull terrier pup into a *raging carnivore*. It wasn't long before the autopsy when they discovered his hidden brain tumour.

Julian Biggs hid in the safety of the kitchen as Tyson sniffed the ground for the olid night-stealer.

With his back to the sink the *pharmacist nervously* giggled. He promised them a share in his scrip if they would only lend him another tenner to go out on the town with.

They badgered the pet into hunting for an evil spirit present in the establishment.

A cracking on the wall convinced the *guardian* of the contagious boil wheezing at the far end.

Fresh from the cold black void where he had crouched waiting for his chance the sturdy breed charged up to the wood where he barked ferociously.

Ryan restrained his *alter-ego* with a grappling-hook around the kronos collar.

"Please, don't ever open the door!" he called to the

Flash.   But it was too late.   An imp had loosened the
catch.

Tyson lunged instinctively forward into the cell.
Julian held his hands up to his throat and caged his
legs inward towards the table top.

"Don't let him get me!" he pleaded pitifully...
In one foul swipe *the grim reaper* from the cellar bit
clean through the debutant's *staypress* and severed all
his wedding tackle.   Gnash! Gulp...

The *big man* was still cantankerous over the dog's
demise.   After attacking Abigail he had pinned it to
the wall with a pitchfork, for which he held her partly
responsible.   Bolted down his dish.

With the gooseberry tucked in the back of the motor
between them he considered how much the drama had cost
in untold damages.   But how long would the honeymoon
period last?   Her iron will wrought across her brow.

All evening the 'twins Narcissus' had been competing
with each other for the audience's admiration, preening
their turgent physiques, and posing as they watched
themselves in the *Room-full-of-mirrors*.

Abigail insisted that he always had to take second
place when ever she attended *the Salty Dog*.   She
professed to hate the sight of men's bodies, but never
seemed able to take her eyes off them.

The puck tickled for the last time inside her ear.
"What did I tell you if you did it again!" she stormed.
His repetition resulted in a black eye for which he
promised to get even with her.

After being locked out of the house for half an hour
it was F. who eventually pulled down the latch.

She blazed fierily upstairs to confront her husband
who was asleep in the bedroom.   She slammed the bedroom
door!   The beauty of her soul seemed to shine through.

F. wandered drowsily to his wanking pit.   Having a
breather was also a pain in the neck due to the
embroidery of *sun spots* which stretched across his
wefted skull.

Naked as the day he was born.

At first it sounded like the removal company. Then the
blast of muffled screams exploded through the
floorboards. Always came back for more.

He pendulously emerged from the 'Outer Limits' to
prick up his ears at the skirling bray.

A blood curdling yell hissed from their chamber.
Abigail was calling him at the top of her powerful
lungs as if it were the end of the world.

Her piercing emanations tootled so pityfully that he
prepared to intervene, although he knew that it might
eventually back-fire.

Her petrified voice booming through the stillness
hollered for the pensive lodger.

He began to tap gently on their now silent panel.
The woman's *consecutive fifths* suddenly reached fever
pitch and puled that Ryan was attempting to make her
gag. Not such a dumb blonde afterall.   Eventually her
husband rose from the floor where she was pinned, to
the fulminating of faecal obscenities, and swaggered
with 'nothing on.' All's fair in love and war!

Abigail rushed past in a veil of tears with her
blonde dye drenched from the washbasin.

Ryan dragged her roughly back by the roots.
"Ere, you've got a police record haven't you?" leered
the drunkard. The atmosphere swiftly shifted to an
even more sudden flashpoint.

"As a matter of fact I have!" reddened the Flash.
He floundered backwards and forwards in a gale. "It's
called 'Message in a bottle!'"

Ryan whispered something vile and rotten to his wife
which F. could only guess at...

"He's a what?" she startled back and tartly pouted.
Suddenly she could only look him in the ghoulies, and
dropped him like a lead balloon. The bra-strap was
hanging over her shoulder. Bet he *wanks about us.*

"Uuuuuuugh! How disgusting," she gasped screwing up
her trick out. She kissed Ryan on his cheek.

"Now he'll never have time for a serious
relationship when news of this gets out!"

"You aren't going to leave me in the parlour with
features!?" she pleaded...really in the dog-house.

'Bet he wanks about us'

The seven o'clock Express to the training course at
Donny had been a matchless exercise in *Bad manners.*

Once alone in the carriage the well-aspected estate
agent was allowed to take a long studious tour of
inspection over his fine listed building.

Despite the obscene comments circulating among the
station staff about which nuthouse he was in residence
F. managed to waltz in through the other side of the
driver. Hubble, bubble, toil, and trouble!

He nipped through the automatic doors and peered
back over the deserted ward.

The bedlamite had missed the intercity Pullman by a
whisker after plonking through his alarm call.

"Where's your ticket twat?" pealed O'Flanagan as he
whistled along platform nine.

F. had not satisfied his rampant urges but the staff
of life was just around the corner...

The L.D.C. monkey-gods scurried from their rocks to
have a good long stare at the oddity.

F. finally found his type on the slow 'milk' train
to school. He was encouraged by her positive body
language which expressed itself in smiles of anxious
anticipation, together with the more subtle
psychological traits of posturing.

Observing her painted reflection in the sun dazzled
glass he pretended to be dozing with an occasional
glance to his left.

His sweat-rag floated high above his *aestival*
erection. Off his bleeding rocker! No doubt about it.

The bloated head sought out the prime-time eyes of
the sex-starved strawberry blonde, as she coyly tugged
her hem, and then dropped her work documents...which F.
leaned awkwardly over to gather. She was full of
gratitude; top marks for gallantry!

The Wankaholic finally scrapped the *aegis* of his
permit to let her eyes feast on the rock hard hump.

On each separate occasion that she was observed
Marlene was almost slavering between her secular
blushes & ...

A dog always returned to his business.

She was gaping open mouthed as he caught her hawking *everhard.* Trust him to focus on that.

The short aisle-way between them was seldom patrolled by the lazy watchman.

He preferred to peek through the break van door just as F. was splattering his load over the seat cover.

The red-hot obsidian almost filled the doorway and seeped in an *elephant's foot* over the step to the touchdown. There was never a bobby around when you needed one! Got his foot in the door.

As he jumped from the moving train Flashman noticed the girl still waiting for him to catch up at the bridge. It was pure fiction, but at least she kept it underneath her bonnet.

The beautiful creature was still blushing madly as he perambulated sentimentally along the gang-plank to the doxy.

The *black dwarf* was waiting outside the entrance tapping impatiently on the casing of his watch-lens.

It had been decided by the bigwigs to mount a campaign to infuse a sense of courtesy in the jobbernowls. It was also to be preferred that they should aspire to an attitude of ordinary politeness.

"You're two minutes late this morning!" he scowled. "You'll definitely be reported to your home depot."

F. entered the classroom with his face flushed by the colour of ichor. It was immediately apparent to everyone that he had been up to some insidious depravity. No matter how much he tried to smoke-screen the disturbance on his skin simply intensified, and he had still to prepare for any possible *ramifications.*

"I've been sprinting like the clappers," he explained. He imbibed like a *fish out of water.*

Ryan passed him a humorous sketch skilfully executed of a vermilion coloured creature with horns and a pointed tail, wearing a mischievous beam. Upon its head were a series of cespitose plugs.

"Mr. Ryan," asked the teacher. "What is the colour of a section stop siganl?"

"Blue!" someone blurted...."Who said that? Who said
that?" asked the teacher, earnestly scrutinizing his
wise men of Gotham.

His glance settled on F. whose *cherry red* had still
not subsided. 'Footlight fever.'

"If I looked like some of you," chuckled the teacher
grinning, "I don't think that I'd dare come outside the
door in the morning..."

"Is it true that you're never going to get a steady
girlfriend? Aren't you ever going to hoover those
green tiles stinking out your bedroom? How can you
ever become *Mr. Universe!* He pointed to his chest.
"You've pulled them down from your head!" he laughed.
And not a squeak was heard.

"You've had a girlfriend before? What, a
prostitue...a whore? I bet you don't even know your
carburetor from your camshaft."

Ryan scoffed impatiently..."If you really want her
that much then attempt a kidnap before somone else gets
their maulers on her!" Ryan was always moaning his
calves did not respond. Dared show his face though.

"At least I don't look like Friar Tuck," he taunted.
"How will you ever be an actor?"

The rest of his lapdogs instantly emulated; "We all
know you're still a little virgin."

Ryan Starbuck stared coldly out of the window.
"Why did you call me 'Bald Eagle'?" queried F.,
resenting and resisting his natural stereo-typing.

"Why on earth do you think!" snapped Ryan aghast,
turning to glare queerly at the embarrassment.

"You've a week to fuck off" he hissed. "Me and
Abigail are emigrating to *Saudi* in the very near
future." Soon to be planning a family.

"If I went without for more than a day I'd be
slipping it in't wrong oyle," he snickered.

When the dinner bell sounded F. made sure he was
first through the exit of the captivity hall. He
helter-skeltered into the main arcade...

Hire a white van before anyone else gets their maulers in!

As the girl at the Western Denim Company handed him the
jeans through the gap of the curtain rail a motley
caste of Beagles arrived into the shop from the sun
drenched precincts.

He was just striking a pose and starching his blue
stocking. "You, on the stage?!!!"

F. paled considerably as he recognized their
household words discussing his probable whereabouts.

"We saw him go in there!" cackled Catweasel...
"No thankyou, but these are not the correct fit..." or
words to that effect...the assistant gagged when she
eye-balled his gobstopper.

"Look at Bald Eagle! What are you doing in there?"
he blasted through the *nullah*. "I wouldn't even
Rottweiler her!"

The quarry froze like a hedgehog caught in the
headlights of their lorry.

She screamed for the men in black to have him
arrested. A mad, bad, mad, bad, world.

"Look at the size of 'it's' hairy chest!" shrieked
the fine *young Cannibal*.

"It's 'Exhibitionists' like you who give
'Bodybuilders' a bad name!" Ryan disparaged.

"He's the last one you want to see doing that sort
of thing," she agreed. '50 years in the wilderness.'

With his head swelling from pride the officer
revealed his nigrescent note-pad.

"He certainly can't score with the chicks...Bald
Eagle fancies himself. It's a pity no-one else does!"

Unless they could find a witness he was going to get
off 'Scot free!'

"Well, why shouldn't she?"
"If she bloody well wants to!"
"I can do what I fucking well like!"

Do turkeys ever vote for Christmas?

the 'Strange little man who stares'

The Reddleman twines in thespian grey
skeined to the fog's iron spokes,
sky peels away as whistle by erica,
at troubled eyes perusing prime thoughts.

On the twisting divan the damsel distress,
sitting down distances, adjusting her dress,
settled at bay in a scissoring spit,
and the core impaled to her script.

The strange little man, gone with the wind,
fidgets and frowns, sinks west if she screams,
prevaricate proud with the world in a cloud
to the strain on her hand soft as swan's down.

Mauve the rine morion of temple orient,
exuberate cross-current over famble scatturent,
the lustreless onanist leans in rapid disgrace,
beneath her ruby red view.

Oh! Rosula of ruth in wasteland rills youth,
blossom with favourable glow,
in jugular reined beside nacaret flame,
one touch, proclaim salts which only are faithful.

Built on Barren Earth in the 'Promised land' of
Purgatory the lonely Signalbox creaked sedately along
the cast-iron skeleton hung with the levers and
Instruments.

For one whole century the clank of the fetch down
below would scrunch among the scaffold of the
Glasshouse roots and beams bedded down in darkness
underwood, as a harbour spleen humped its raincoat on a
hook by the sneak.

In the slim House of detention confinements of space
were furnished with wooden planks, like an interred
hulk, but not planted in the slimey juices of briny...

Ancient bloodfeud suspended talk-talk among the
alienated castaways for years over a rude trifle
involving nothing but small beer. Which meant the
parties would play it by the rules for awkwardness
sake, and *call attention* every single time to give the
'Train-out-of-Section!' bell-signal.

All the prisoners in exile had their queer
preferences, and the strange Baboon *of Boetia* was no
exception. Cabin fever!

This odd fogy moidered on the brink of dotage, nay,
who would dare to call him potty, was the ass in a
lion's skin responsible for those cranky drafts
scribbled on such diverse subjects as the greenhouse
effect and the possible uses of spellbinding.

What a fiasco there had been within the packed
meeting room of the *Green person* that nearby noon, with
reporters waiting in the wings for signs of dolthood,
when Ernest had rose to promulgate his opinion on the
imminent strike call. Could he still jaunt in to
nourish his marrows?

Brother 'Proudtoe,' standing rank among three union

pinheads like Triton among the minnows, and sweating
indecently in his ill fitting suit straight from the
peg, proudly held the copy of the _Shipping forecast_
high in the air.

Sporting a severe middle-age paunch he mopped his
brow in desperation, and declared the vote unanimous on
a show of hands.

F.'s first fear was that he might assume a partial
likeness if he stayed in the Plague City until
saturation point.

He consciously avoided copying any of their
mannerisms and vowed never to become a regular cave-
dweller...

The tall Boetian stood to greet him at the door and
tapped his clay madder pipe on the side of the bench
where a mound of ash had clogged. His washing was
spread round the flame.

His turn-ups were rolled up his shins and his size
twelve pugs were steaming in the hot tin bowl to soothe
his gout.

The Signalman's snow white hair was tinged with a
smear of copper and a thin brown line traced along the
outer fringes of his coaming.

Ernie described in eloquent detail the day he had
seen a U.F.O. flying up the valley towards him.

In a dramatic tink he disclosed how the object had
rocketed up the channel of the railway line, suddenly
accelerating and increasing its velocity like no
earthly craft.

"I thought it was a cattle-truck when it first
appeared flashing its green lights in the distance," he
chuffed. "And I was going to send seven bells to
Linus, who was just finishing his landscape of the
Cotswolds in the shippen."

"Then it came at me! Veering towards the rain-
forest. They were the strangest crew I've ever seen
(and I've seen a few!). His hand was waving as the
ship flew over the banking. Then I noticed Scargill
glaring through the bubble."

He walked angularily to the portal where the moped
rider would drape himself with the olive green mac and
furnace goggles, throwing on his baldric and hob nailed
boots, before preparing to hike it up the steep meadow
still in his PJ's...the scarf tied over his head gave
one the impression of a Bunny.

In oblate seconds the twenty-two stone
Brobdingnagian entered and angrily slammed the door in
his wake.

It was a charm watching him attempt to dismount from
his three-wheeler on the brow of the lane.

The walrus hair sprouting from his nostril could
have easily been culled into a brush. Floss seemed to
spring from his every orifice. Never had a day on the
sick his mate said.

Anus had a bird's nest growing in his beard. He
even appeared to be suffering from a deficiency of
calcium. The relief was a natural supporter of the
Gunners. He never swabbed his purple-and-white neck-
rope.

"He's a dirty old twat!" he snapped.
The *Relief Box-man* raced straight over to the traces of
ash on the floor where old Ernest had happily tapped
his ancient tool, and blew his top. Flung open a case
of his gaspers.

With his shirt tail still remonstrating over his
enormous buttocks he lumbered over to the Block Bells.

He acknowledged the 3.1 for the passenger train on
the solid brass tapper key before swinging the
apparatus to 'Is Line Clear,' while studying the going
form – flat to firm.

He passed the officer's special waiting in the
station to the Junction, which was acknowledged by
3.55, for which he placed a 'reminder appliance' on the
starter signal, before taking out his television set to
watch the results.

Ignoring the trainee who might rob him of his *rest-
day working*, the scruff, with bran still hanging to the
underside of his belly, reported the time and unit
number to "Plank" on the traffic control switchboard.

He cracked open his bottle of Stout before turning the
armchair away from the unwanted guest floundering like
a needle in a bottle of hay.

The Kraken emerged from the Booking Office to go to
the thunderbox at the end of the platform.

He was a smartly dressed man in his mid-fifeties who
always wore a clean white shirt and tie, an unmarried
batchelor in the village.

Anus drew attention to the wanderer who had already
paid several visits to the MEN'S that afternoon, and
was once again blithely strolling down the platform
beneath the flowerbaskets oblivious of their eyes
scrutinizing him from the quadrangle.

"Watch this dirty git will you!" he huffed. "Every
time there's some 'kiddies' playing on the station he's
in and out of there like a don't know what."

Sure enough a pack of boy scouts were playing
chicken near the platform edge.

After a few minutes _the_ Kraken came out 'doing up
his flies' and self-consciously patting his podgy
waistline. The 'Kraken' smiled as the daleks pretended
to _exterminate_...made invisible!

The booking clerk did glance slyly up at the
Signalbox but the glass put a glare in his lens.

He'd be back again every ten minutes to loiter in
the freight inlet and stare along the sunset strip
while polishing his frame.

The unfriendly _Ground Sloth_ rose from his rocker to
pull-off the soft metal end of the rod with the aid of
an old rag. He yanked the _dolly_ for his Crossover.

"You'll be coming out with us on Thursday!" he
slapped assuredly.

"When ya tekkin owwer? Sidney Wheel has gi-un us
the word," grunted Anus.

"Thass'll be striking with the rest of the brothers
to bring this Tory scum to a halt! They've bin nothing

but trouble to the _hewers of wood and drawers of water_."

"I really don't think so!" squared the Flash. "Anyway I haven't really made my mind up yet. But I think Mrs. T. is doing a grand job. Without Maggie we'd be a nation of atrabilious shop stewards and gay tin gods."

The melinomic ground sloth towering over him raised his arm as if to strike F. dead, and then convened the coup on thinking better of it, staring down in deep astonishment at the upstart.

He was searching desperately for an expression with which to pigeon-hole him. A back-formation he could conveniently pin on the pest. Anus began frothing at the mouth. Tiny red oxygen bubbles infuscated his gums among the sharp incisive mandibles.

"You do know who I am?" he seethed authoritively. "Tha knows I'm t'h Union Sec'rtry for this area...that's all!"

The Sloth caught F. educing his lineament and for some reason assumed he was inclining him into a moss-back. His prognathous jaw snapped like a crocadile handbag. Neanderthal man was alive and kicking in Britan...

"If ya does come into work," smirked Anus, sneering with the _thunders of the Vatican_. "then I'd 'ave ya guts for garters. That would make you a scab, a _blackleg_, and I'd make damn sure ya never worked anywhere round here agen..."

As the train passed through the oriel below he casually gave the 2.1 (Train-Out-of-Section) signal to Henry Furnace at the Junction, slung the signal lever back to danger, and replaced the Block Instrument gauge to _Normal_.

"Why don't you just go and crawl back under whatever stone it is you've just crept out from," he hollered menacingly, and smashed F.'s beaker bad-temperedly on the clodge.

Departing the brick lifting competition at the sports
stadium packed with human beings of the 'Twenty-first
century,' where the 'Strongest man in the world' was
acting as compere, accompanied by his lovely hostess,
the Flash twirled his 'First World War' fighter pilot's
moustache, and parked his Triumph Spitfire at the
entrance, examining the harsh indentations over the
wheel arch, shaped like the excesses of a crude stone
pestle.

They say that every life has its typical experience,
so we can only become more dismayed when we hear how he
was able to get away with it for such a very long
innings...

Boarding the club-car at the *Terminus*, where the
senior grouse slinked right up by his side, F.
determined to use the first free miles of his travel
allowance.

The noon-day train was always a safe bet. Sure
enough he found her sitting pretty at the extreme of
the rear carriage, constructively contemplating the
epithet of 'modern living.'

As the turning wheels began to rattle westwards the
dark attractive 'Nightingale' offered him one of her
Liquorice Alsorts. 'Must flog more 'Cheap Day Singles','
he thought.

F. had just bought a bag of fresh strawberries and
gave her one in return.

The fruit was a little *bitter* to the taste, but this
was of no consequence to a creature who could devour
stardust.

He started to emancipate the teeth of his chattering
zipper to prepare an introduction with his sleeping
accomplice. Anyone for tennis?

"Not without double cream," she winced as he offered
her another enticement. Philomena continued with the
chart of her voyages.

The young woman travelling with the Preserver began
to fidget too as he carefully ascertained whether the
greedy eyes of the grey haired spinster were in harvest
of his *treasure trove*.

He began to force the puppet into the wide open field,
far more deliberately and daringly than ever before.
Each deviant act re-inforcing his odd pathology. The
student nurse quivered at the _operating table_...
     She seemed desirous to discuss the need for common
purpose, but our man had more pressing ideas to cope
with. Too brief to form an attachment?
     The passive eyes turned increasingly towards the
brim of the book cover to face him, as they passed the
huge phallic tower of 'Kings Cross' with its immense
masonic glans. To be honest their current relationship
remained on the whole _rather_ limited though.
     Once again the deviant carried on the show for much
longer than he need have. Her bleary buds eventually
relaxed silently on the quintain and settled down to
watch with rising adulation. Without another word she
slowly followed the 'X' certificate, and cocked an eye
sharply on his _thalamus_, although the plot was almost
undecipherable, she gulped and regurgitated all her
grub..(in an out 'a there!
     His _utopian urge_ buttered like a sunflower under the
spray of saffron bleaching from behind the welt of
cloud...he really must consider _circumcision_...the
fulsome smell overcame the farmer's cram. His
buttermilk rose to the surface. Blocks of stardust.
     With the diesel coming gradually to a holt beneath
the station canopy, filled with the summer primroses
swinging rhythmically in their seasonal baskets of
straw, the strange little man began ejaculating in
syncopation with the application of the squeaking curb.
The station master gloared with the watering can static
in his grasp./j(O-nly 'jesturing!'
     Suddenly he noticed Shittlegruber lurching on the
bench with 'his' replacement.
     The old _Lampman_ was unable to contain his disgust.
He turned to distract his colleague's attention. With
his finger shaking nervously he pointed sheepishly
toward a silver body laden in the azure firmament.

No matter how F. tried to stem his flow, until 'kingdom
come' he continued to spurt his oily semen around the
cowshed walls, finally running out of canvas.

While the 'chestnut mare' hummed the _Cuius Animam_ he
attempted to disguise his extraneous seed. The odd-
jobber climbed down from his ladder and came to peer
with astonishment through the adjacent window. Then
sighing at his feet she even had the temerity to
importune him for his digits. Make believe.

Pressing his _mufti_ against the offending place F.
managed to make it to the gangway and perambulated
alongside the coaches of the seaside special.

Camouflaging the magic drops of ambrosia in whose
potency and profit our very life depends the clockwork
fool loped mechanically along the distant platform to
the 'detention centre' of the pale green Glasshouse
perched on the flange of the pier.

A 'man-in-black' emerged from the station concourse.
"Who's that?- 'The Signalman!'" Of course.

In the certain knowledge that he would be foregoing
his former ally on the _down_ F. prayed for the hollow
earth to swallow him up. There was nothing about
Dorian a paper bag could not fix.

Assaulted by the circumambience of electric hemlock
F. approached the other home with his zip still only at
half mast. If he tampered around the region further,
people were liable to become suspicious.

Once inside the den he had hours to contemplate the
homeward journey on which to brandy his fettles. He
would just have to learn to be more patient.

Through the looking glass flickering images of the
fist fuck rigadooned like shadows on the interior, but
Walt and his Missus were nowhere to be seen.

Anchored on a rock his spawn drowsed woodenly at the
scene. Every air hole in the stuffy cabin was tightly
blocked. Al-fiction.

F. alighted nimbly over the shining hum of lines and
noted the brand new sailing dingy moored resplendently
at the bottom of the well-worn steps – a present from

the head of livestock. Walts tin motor was harnessed
down in mud.

He banged his feet noisily against the nadir of the
loft to give them time to climax before climbing to the
top. He knocked on the windowpane marked 'Private'
before pressing down the metal catch with a loud click.

A young man with a basin cut of raven hair was
hastily adjusting his shirt while his auburn haired
seamstress combed her hair in the mirror.

The brats remained completely motionless and
continued to monitor the crescendo point on the screen.

Maxine rolled her dream clad eyes and touched her
face still flushed from prolonged pairing.

Her drifting palps ploughed half cocked through the
thrushes of her locks. She stared straight forward
towards the door as F. immediately retired to the _Train
Register Book_ in order to sign on duty.

Walt grinned and replaced the knotted white
handkerchief on his swollen summit. He informed F.
that he was 'back with the missus' now that the charge
nurse had given him the slip.

Walter blushed and stared curiously down at the
traces of _albumen_ still sticking stubbornly to the
arena of F.'s filthy fastener.

"I think you ought to know," he said. "The
Signalmen in this area are gabbing about you all day
long! It's embarrassing! I have to work with him I
told them..." One mans' plight, is another mans's delight!

The _family of fugitives_ gathered their belongings
and piled into the hill-billy van while F. opened the
brown paper parcel which had been flung from the
Junction library. Out of his tree! (o)...

The ex-booking lad had an unsettling habit of
practically rubbing noses while he jaw-jawed, although
useful tips of sound practical advice were gratefully
accepted by the raw recruits.

An avowed athiest until his daughter's recent
heroine overdose, which he blamed on the evil excesses
of the inimical modern era, the _verandah tinkerer_ had
become a staunch advocate of the Rosicrucians.

Now he clubbed along the signalling frame every morning before the golden dawning of the sun.

An article on blatant showing-off proved to be an interesting _stocking-filler_, but from where the Signalman reclined in his _deck chair_ he could observe the engrossing antics of the local pedestrians as they flowed along the winding path towards the local factories over the river.

It was not a _dazzling Pharos_ on the quiet sea coast, but the peculiar ambience of the outlandish glaciated valley had a monastic charm of its own, and would provide a suitable retreat until the treatment had been done away with.

The _Bridge_ nestled in the shaded crux of the Cedar trees, where strange fogs emerged at midnight and _wyrd_ auditory effects echoed through the besmirched Utopia among the watering-place.

'Black-balled,' he stood up in his red bathing costume as the youthful traffic of souls filed past on their way home from elementary learning.

A _piccolo utterance_ issuing eternally from the poultry farm on the strangulated hernia of the hill. Under the Railway Bridge below the station cottage one could distinguish their isolated screams...

Away in the fields through an arc of the evergreen F. could elucidate a couple copulating in the grass. A party of schoolchildren peered through the broken fencing.

It was the middle of July; the bluebottles were always in plentyful supply attracted by the poultry pipe. At this time of year the billion or so eggs began to hatch in the dry sultry heat, and the _alien nation_ were constantly having migraine.

Hanging on the aviary railing outside the box was a bag of roasted peanuts...a hawker had been pestering him for half an hour as he nourished himself with their contents.

Had him weighed up in two bleeps. From the time I first set eyes on him!

YOU ONLY GOT SEVEN YEARS FOR MURDER!

If you were male...

It could have been a 'train spotter.' There were
plenty of _anoraks_ knocking about the station embankment
during holidays. Some of them even asked if they could
see inside the Greenhouse. Ogger United!!
     Eventually the 'fugleman' sidled up to the low wall
and asked if the earnest romancer was on the payroll.
     "I'm sorry, no-one of that name!" smirked the
Flasher. "What's the matter now? He owes you
cash...am I right?!"

The bloodred sunset turned suprisingly sharply into
Stygian darkness, with the flash of lightning rattling
up the glade and heading most of all for the desolate
cabin.
     Within minutes of the 'Flagman' setting down his
tackle for the 'Engineer's Possession' the bolts of
thunder were striking furiously on the roof and rapping
on the door knob.
     As a thick downpour of hail began to flail the
clover-leaf a brawling couple _caterwauled_ from the
public house over the slippery ford.
     'Dirty Dick' arranged the detonator protection on
the twinkling surface of the rail-head and erected his
red flags at either extremity. He asked for permission
to place a bogie on the line.
     As the wind began to howl the 'Pilotman' wearing his
red and yellow armband arrived by the last train to put
in 'single line working.' He was also the 'Person-in-
charge-of-the-Possession!'
     Wars of the elements were always summoned by decree
to the Glasshouse.
     Even though the box had a lightning conductor safely
rooted to earth the _raider_ made a special effort to
remain overhead in the black Kipling sky.
     Dick settled himself down in the corner for a kip
before reaching for the literature nearest to hand.
     "E', just think lad!" he chuckled. "At this precise
moment there will be some young lass bending down to
gobble her mate for the very first time."

The old chap was covered in a proliferation of facial scars, and had been hit three times by locomotives while working on the _Permanent way_. He had once been a fireman on the footplate of the 'Titfield thunderbolt.'

"When ya numbers up, ya numbers up!" he swagged, chomping and sucking on his gums.

Dick pricked scornfully at his steel capped boot resting on the parapet.

"One on em even ran ower me toe!" he roared. "But he mun't ad mi name on it!"

A caber of inductance crashed through the open valance causing palpitations.

He raised his hammer about to strike the clock and began lashing drunkenly askew.

When he finally stood firm Barnacle Bill retold that tale about his national service days on the Ganges.

_He_ narrated how he had returned to barracks one afternoon to discover the squadron hall completely empty.

After some earnest searching around he had heard cheering ringing from deeper in the _vellum_...where some of the company were going back for 'second helpings' with the eleven year old 'Arian' concubine.

In minutes he was in the _land of Morpheus_ with a few loose pages falling from his gripe...

When the telephone rang F. was not at all surprised to hear Ryan Starbuck calling from Gehenna.

"Who've you seen this week besides your relief?" he teased. "Have you been in any more trouble yet?"...He uttered the expletive 'Kidnap' and then the line went dead for no apparent reason. It seemed engaged.

Suddenly a thick band of ochre came shooting through the oven door like the nemesis limb of Thunor, and thumped powerfully on the brass knob of the tapper key giving the Flasher an unexpected shock! The cobalt groaned with glitter from the veins of _Mjollnir_. But it was _only god trying to take his mugshot_.

After a longer than expected deliberation in which he had twice threatened to run for home F. sauntered to

the entrance of the Wasteland in the calm of the
bereaved storm.

A rustle of twigs sizzled where the hungry *Beast*
stood shivering below the mantle of silver birch. He
had certainly built-up a head of steam.

On the strait patch of ground which trickled from
the surrounding scud a creature miraculously appeared
and stamped its hoof impatiently on the sodden mound of
turf.

The *Flash* tottered in amazement, magically
transported by the wavering spell of 'liberty'...he
smiled and tried to neutralize the migrant with the
soft concord of truce.

In the cool mist of midnight, wrapped by the
overhanging sprigs of spinney, the inner sense of the
Thunderbuck Ram had wandered freely from the tranquil
slopes, in a hiss of scraping pebbles.

In a rare moment of calm the envoy's sap met his
eyes as the hot hart breath ejected from his steaming
nostrils like a censer smoke.

F. stood in the doorway hardly daring to move in
case he bolted into *ether*. The scout stood listening
to his every single syllable hypnotized by poppy. He
became conscious of the warbling of the heavens. The
stronger the song the greater the element. His soft
waters floated over turbulence...and situated below his
forehead were two amethysts.

'Before the hartless fall of Adam I bound the Yews of
Anderida; for I love all that is pure and in my
resurrection reigns supreme.

Beyond the North wind I panned the second wall of
ice. The thorn that never fades away.

I was drowned in a sea of fractious malice.
My saddle toasted figureheads at the table. I split
the shafts of my immurament.

Nine great obscurities on the storm-tossed larch.
On the sixth day I died and was taken in. Out of
darkness I wondered from the chill.

Whiffled by the four corners of the world I suckled you
at my pearl. For I was greater than the follies of
your youth. Summer poured from my mouth.
                Sorrow poured from my hearth.
From the forest fringe I swept your tiny cove across
the bleeding lung to the shoreline.
    My leaking beads beneath the Great Solferino stared
into the face of a glaring mammoth.
    Yes, I flew in the coin of an arrow. With a star,
and a crescent, we were able to scale the heights.
    I will weather the storm, stem the tide and reap the
fruits over all the kingdoms of my earth.
    Where there is floruit I will bring weir for all the
Sons of Uprooted Gaels. For lover's Supreme /
    The chords of my hymn had been trampled into dust.
For I am the beast of morphic
resonance...'

The Flashman suddenly hearkened, and found himself
still staring into the early morning dawn with the
church bells on the apex tintibullating vehemently. He
offered up the Yule-log. Antler scored palm!   A cock
was crowing as *Anus* stomped across the threshold...
laid out on the deck were the ten obstreperous members
of the *tamping* gang who had evacuated the paddle.

The refugees from the flood had gathered wearily for
shelter on the wooden tree stump of the landscape.

    "*C'est la vie!*" he shrugged. "But not as we know
it..."

    "If I ever catches who put those bloody *bluebottles*
in my ham sandwich I'm going to crucify him," barked
Anus.

F. felt for the clavis to the glass cage which was
normally hidden under the step, and opened the door, on
his second turn of duty.

    It had been cleaning day alright, but the Signalbox
floor was covered in debris from the dustbin.

    His locker had been burst open and all the contents
had been systematically covered in black tar from the

53

bunker, with a conglomeration of rotting vegetables
heaped on the armchair.

The chrome training bench had vanished without
trace, and the iron barbells had disappeared or were
beaten brutally out of shape. It would be a long while
until he could continue with his French curls.

A mysterious note was scribbled on the writing pad
addressed to the 'nadir man.' Since he had been sent
to _Coventry_ the clique constantly referred to him as
the 'Screwball.' It simply meant a longer spell out of
circulation. *Stylites Simon.*

Just as he was turning towards the booking office he
suddenly noticed the 'Area Inspector' sneaking at warp
speed up the swathe of undergrowth on his blind side.

The hunter quickly entered the signalbox in three
swift bounds instantly accusing F. of being indecently
dressed.

The Inspector was wearing a consumptive grey suit
which he fitted like a pipe cleaner's coathanger.

"Don't let me see you without your shirt again!"
rebuked the 'Chinless Wonder' sternly.

"You must wear your issued uniform every time you
are on duty."

"Balderdash!" snapped the Flash. "Are you jealous?"
The man responded sharply. Had the grip of a Short
Grandmaster.

"It's Mr. Stretch to you!" in a high pitched wail of
an utterance...was he a eunuch?

"I've heard enough bad reports about _you_ from your
fellow mates. Not a day goes by when there is not
another rumour. If your behaviour towards them does not
improve I'll have no option but to drag you into the
Area Manager's Office to give you a grilling on the
rules!"

"Look at the disgusting state of this Shit-tip!"
complained the Chinless wonder, clucking his Adams'
apple _vigilantly._

"It never used to be like this until you got here."
He suggested that F. had caused the _pretty kettle of
fish_ himself when he disclosed that _Anus_ had been there
just before him.

"Though I'm glad to see you've eventually decided to
remove your training bench," he conceded.

Well aware of their attitude towards strangers F.
attemped to conceal his blackened transistor before he
could get a whiff of it. There was an era when even
the reading of newspapers was not permitted. But the
Inspector's gimlet swooped on the _boot-legging_ like a
bird of prey when he was that way out.

"You closed that door as if you had a dead body
inside," whimpered the deleterious Inspector. "Let me
have a look! You know Mr. Greenwood's attitude towards
anything crooked." Better not mention Bernadette's _pot
plants_ then...

The charlatan stared aghast, but F. eventually
persuaded him that the gadget was only a 'heart-beat
monitor.'

"This is a very responsible job!" he insisted. "The
most responsible on the railway. If I ever catch you
with a radio on it'll be a form one and you'll be shown
the door!"

Thank god for small blessings...He hinted that the
dole queue stretched for miles.

"Why were two trains stood for half an hour on
either side of the station the other day?"

"Anus refused to relieve me at the regular time but
sat reading his _Morning Star_ on the platform while I
walked to my car. Why don't you arrange the rosters so
we never have to meet? It should easily be possible."

"Oh, I don't want to know about your silly
bickering," he cried, "and don't start telling me my
terms of reference or you'll be on a hiding to
nothing."

The Inspector scratched at the cream enamel surface
of the cooker top and took out his magnifying glass.
'There was no need to make a mountain out a molehill,'
he said.

"The whole place has fallen into disrepute," he
flustered joyfully. "Look at the ring marks on the
floor, it's a blinking eye-sore!"

The Area Inspector shifted his glance craftily towards
the periodicals.

"How long is it since you read your 'Rules and
Regs?'" he schemed.   Then suddenly..."What's a 2.6.2
bell signal?" he screamed, trying to catch him with his
pants down.

"A 'Train which cannot be allowed to pass trains
similarily signalled or signalled 2.6.3, on the
opposite or adjoining line!" sparked the Flash.

So quickly and without hesitation that the Chinless
wonder jumped in the air.

His prominent Adams apple Yo-Yo-ed perniciously like
a disagreeable turkey cock.

"Incidentally Mr. Stretch, before you go," snapped
the Flash.   "What would be the consequence of someone
having a television set on the job, and using *Great
Western* fuel to finance his flutter?"

"*Instant dismissal!*" snapped the Inspector
belligerently and with absolute certainty.

The chinless wonder cleared his throat about to
declaim his 'coup-de-grace,' after warning him about
'ringing in' the units as they approached so the
platform staff could be ready to leap out from the
subway.

"There's one other small thing," he smiled, with a
fraudulent gleam in his frivolous eyes...

"Your regular mate has made a serious complaint
about your improper conduct.   He says that you have
pinched his nuts!"

The Flash had to momentarily demur.   Had there
indeed been an impropriety somewhere along the line?

"Certainly not!" he declined. "I did no such thing!
I've always kept my hands strictly to myself..."

He observed the Area Inspector stroll blithely down
the length of yard.   He'd promised to return the
following day at six a.m. but F. suspected it was just
another ruse.

The Inspector patted his old chum on the shoulder
and warmly stroked his mawler.   They turned to gaze up

at the pillar of the monatomic unit where the sentence
was held in perennial execution. The two began to
guffaw.

F. dimmed all the lights and turned the mirror
against the wall. Strange the Inspector not mentioning
his capture of the burgular, caught red-handed climbing
a ladder through the booking office porthole...

With nothing better to do he flicked the switch of
the circuit-phone, where the _Flapper_ could gauge their
gabbling non-stop until noon. He could easily discern
the individual baritone clarity of the clones as they
discussed the principles of car mechanics and the
prospects for increased overtime.

Anus began criticizing the antics of the _kithless_
Wrecker who had painted the whole establishment black
as November. He had ended his destructive masterpiece
with the salamander symbol of Aries, scrolled in rust
over the burnished doorway, before smashing up the
block bells and instruments with a crow-bar.

During the long hours spent in isolation _Angus Darke_
had refused to turn the knob for any outside
influences. Ever since his mother's recent demise the
single tenant had become more and more withdrawn,
culminating in his arrest on a minor shop-lifting
charge which had triggered-off a severe bout of
depression.

On the night of the tempest he had pulled-off for
the last newspaper train before retiring down the
treadway. A final cigarette as he sat resting on the
rail bar in the moonlight was all he could muster to
perk his spirits.

"So there he was!" chuckled Anus. "When I came up
the steps he was lying at the side like a sack 'a dirty
old spuds!"

"Bully should be alright for his _rest day_ working
now....his 'Box' must have really gone! I don't see
why anyone should be lonely in this day and age."

The clan decided how best to carve up the spoils...
"I had a mate picked his nose once!"

"One day he discovered that he'd picked all't lining
out of his cap!"

"I knew his brother," nagged the 'Riddler.' "He
caught the same habit and one day his head caved in!"
They all laughed.

The clamour of their wagging tongues continued
without desinence...but it was not long until they
returned to their most favourite topic.

Anus suggested his gear might end its days on top of
the village bonfire.

He gleefully recalled the time when the empty
coaching stock units had been left to stand longer than
was necessary in the sidings, as they attempted to keep
him vapouring, while laughing up their sleeves.

The regular 'Union Treasurer,' pedalling his
bachelor-of-science in systematic knowledge, always
gave them a comprehensive report of the Flashman's
ineptitude at the beginning of every shift.

He whispered like an old tart in a pub doorway about
the day F. had missed his home station.

"And there he was!" chuckled the fellow with the
face like the back of a tram smash. "I didn't hardly
recognize him at first. As the train stood below me in
the blasted platform."

"Flashing away he was, in broad daylight. I could
hardly believe my eyes!"

Once more the heavy crew broke into unbridled mirth
at the top of their vocal chords and a waspish silence
rapidly ensued.

"Do you reckon he's flapping now?" hissed Furnace.
"Let's give him a buzz to see if he's awake..."

Blip/ Blip, B-l-e-e-p! went the whistle of the cable
calling the code of the Bridge. F. flicked his button
because he knew they would hear it click. For once
they seemed to be talking sense.

Had he really heard all that? Should he confront
them immediately and ask them what he meant? The
stripling decided to appear in blissful ignorance and
started on the line as if he had not been 'earwigging.'

58

"Ere, Muscles," answered Anus coolly. The other twelve
dozen candidates listened many miles apart in eager
anticipation.

"You can take on line for this 'un leaving me for
thee. And I thought you'd like to know," he jested
wickedly. "There's an attractive blonde guard in the
rear brake van with her head hanging out of the window
having a *good* look out."

"Why don't you give her a *good flash* as she slows
down...?"

With this remark an eruption of uproarious abuse
echoed down the fathoms of incongruous chamber.

"Well, why don't you try tucking in your smelly
shirt for a change?" rifled the Flash. "What about
Bermondsey then!" he jeered.

"Thas a bit of a tart thaself!" nattered Anus.
Oblivious of the fingernails still lying camouflaged in
the white granules of his sugar bowl.

UPON MY TANGLED MAIN A TRAIL OF STARS SPANGLED FROM THE
TROUGH

"Come-on, ya' boring stick-in-the-mud. Why don't ya'
shift ya' fat arse and 'do' something?"

#   #   #   #

The huge black dome of Bernadette's bushy bonnet rocked
pendulously above the frail cervix of his insignificant
insect body as he counted out the moribund seconds of
his shift...

"Forty-thousand and one, forty-thousand and two,
forty-thousand and three"...He carefully watched the
iron handle of the antique Victorian carriage clock,
which they were starting to replace with quartz crystal.

As he lifted his children's tricycle under his arm
Anus lumbered round the metallic gate at the end of the
station dead on time. Collated anything shiney.

He retrieved his gardening fork from the side of the
door intending to walk over to his family allotment by
the river when the 'chin-chin' was finally done. He
was also President of the local branch of 'Militant,'
so there were other extant worries on his mind.

The *Ground Sloth* clambered with difficulty over the
edge of the platform. His feet stuck in the glue of
the tar where the funicular passage was sign-posted
over the duck-boards.

"Good day brother," grinned the Abbot as he entered
the Wendy house.

"Good day to you too brother!" smiled the conspirator
as they whispered in sly collusion.

Bernadette pointed regretfully to the waste bucket
of rotting vegetables which had accumulated in his
absence...You had to hand it to him.

With a fierce expression the Ground Sloth charged
across the length of the lino and up-braided the
offending article like a mad rogue elephant. He tore
the chair back and tossed it across the space, before
setting on the bone of so much bad feeling and throwing
it rancorously through the open fissure.

Like an exploding bomb the volant tin bucket landed
in the middle of the grass spilling the contents of its
carcass in all directions among the cinders and ash.

Calmly, the logical neurotic trotted over the hum of
the railhead and strode down the platform with his
basket of turnip, and tricycle.

He hesitated at the doorway of the waiting room
where the 'trouble-maker' was being interviewed about
the 'very serious incident,' and dangled crossly at the
ingress. A group of Hutterites danced in their clogs.

"Bit old for one of those aren't you?" snapped the
Flash. He also passed a comment that there were still
living organisms trapped inside the Vegan's lettuce
even after it had been run under the tap.

"Shit-head!" niggled Bernadette bitterly through the
embarcation point and turned to walk briskly to his
lovely Benedick. Practically !

The Flash withered in a mortal funk. Was his career
in jeopardy? Had there been a death on the roads? The
plot thickened...could there have been a fly in his
primeval soup? Could hold his own with anyone.

The Inspector in the moth-eaten cloth scrutinized
him weirdly and folded his arms on the beam of
officialdom. Had a lot of 'hands-on' experience.

With white silk gloves he punctuously unveiled a
small meticulously prepared brown fulscap from his
briefcase and humbly expunged the *presumptive deponent*
to lie in condemnation on the sill.

As F. tottered on the rickety wooden chair he drew a
circle in red around the area of so much marasmus.
Would he have been better employed somewhere else?
We can only hazard a guess...

"Was it you who carried out this vicious assault?"
he issued sternly, pointing to the copy of the
previous months 'Ixion Review,' which had been found
shredded and hanging in the Cabin-de-thunder.

F. glanced nervously down at the monochrome
photograph of *Buck-jaw* happily embracing his allies.
Positioned below the migerous banner their arms were
held aloft in victory celebration.

But someone had deliberately distorted the clan's
expressions with the help of an Indian rubber creating
a gruesome army of conscripts.

"I've also interviewed your regular mate about this
disturbing episode and he is quite certain that they

61

are your finger marks smudging the white edges of the
border," he elaborated.

"I will give you one *final warning!* End your
childish behaviour and put your 'house in order.' If
you do not limit your activities to work routine in a
charitable and more tolerant attitude towards your
fellow members, then we will have no alternative but to
dismiss you from the service!"

VI

MOBY DICK

Like an empty relic from those halcyon days she stood
at the entrance of the *Old Schooner* and bounded over
the capstan with the agility of a young gazelle. She
peeked shyly inside the cockpit still holding her
lobster coloured face with giant claws and deposited
the pint of bitter from the Captain's table.

Jo had returned from phoning the albatross of a
floating world and appeared desperate to become
seaworthy. Inhabitants of the moors eyed her with wild
suspicion. Despite her indomitable 'Atlantean'
strength her goose-flesh was as soft as butter.

"Are you taking me down for a drink?" she asked, and
hunched her huge broad shoulders snugly to his side.
Though she had already demonstrated how much her dorsum
could overlap he still floated in a sea of doubt.

A passing landlubber waltzing his dog under the
street lamp made her keel over and throw her bun of
tawny hair straight between his limbs.

Her lovely knees were parked against the dashboard
and she remarked how the Svengali had suggested she try
walking the boardwalk.

"Don't look at me," she said. "French kissing makes
me feel dirty. I haven't known you long enough.
Perhaps when I feel less nervous, although I can't say
that I really fancy you."

She had nearly reached high tide, but their 'special
relationship' had still remained unconsumated. The
young woman fretted that her best friends were already
on the Pill, and she hadn't even been deflowered at
fifeteen. The Sand-fairy had married a submariner.
Her brother had been poached by a Roc.

"I'm so shy," she said. "You'd tell me if you
didn't like me, wouldn't you? I wept buckets when you

left. Please don't think I'm just using you...don't
you ever take your cap off?"

The girl was sweetly bathed in wisdom but felt
handicapped in her peer group. She had a good self
image and never questioned her right to succeed. He
rested on his oars again.

Skulking like a tiny trawlerman beside her the Flash
could not decide whether to use his harpoon...all she
would feel was a pin-prick, or draw in the net.

He was still fond of the dream but why couldn't she
have remained in the flinder league.

'I would if I could, but I can't,' he mused, and
tried to place his manly arm around her cargo.

"I just lack confidence," she said, but the 'Flash'
was unable to drop anchor.

"Do you think I could be a dyke?" she signalled.
She turned to face him beside the pristine chapel as
they docked at *Gracelands*.

Jo promised to give him a ring when she arrived home
from school the next day but he secretly rescinded.

She had already booked a flight to Geneva where she
intended to join the footlights.

"But Jo-anne, you're six foot four and still
growing!" her boyfriend insisted.

"That's nearly one foot taller than me. I know
'you' don't mind but 'I' don't know how to come to
terms with that."

Mighty Jo Young alighted nimbly from the Spitfire
and bounded deep into the mysterious forest.

"It doesn't matter," she called. "I'm used to being
given the elbow."

When the rank 'Outsider' arrived at the lonely
Glasshouse from his studio shoebox Millie and Lucy were
even now waiting in earnest at the big wall, and were
holding a discarded biscuit tin in their fevered grasp.

He had been tossing and turning all night...
As he climbed the steps Old Boxer was already
slithering down the other end of the platform to his

three wheeler without a single word; residents in the
neighbourhood were beginning to talk in hushed
whispers. The clerk peered down the yard to see what
was going on up in the sentence place.

The children chuckled excitedly as they followed him
out of bounds. It had been many years since he had
last recruited members, but by this time the 'Flash'
could sense a storm brewing.

"Trick or treat?" They implied it was 'Spend-a-
penny' week for the local brownie pack.

"We've brought you some 'eaglet' eggs to look after
until they hatch," sniffed one of the followers. She
pulled the cotton wool aside and presented them for
assessment. The Signalman reckoned on they were
starlings.

"Then we can keep coming back to visit you," giggled
Millie.

Lucy plashed a message to her older accomplice as
the letcher leaned to gaze into the swaddling. He
counted the number of their offspring to be three. A
holy trinity. Seven for a secret never to be t——

"Only if you toss a coin!" he snapped, grinning like
the Wolf. The elves glanced at each other and simply
burst out laughing.

"She's been having rude dreams about you in bed,"
smiled Millie. "I'll do it if you like, but who'll
stand on watch for us?" The girls were already
jostling in collusion.

Malcolm Mondale was inconveniently emerging from
under the Booking Office pavilion.

In seconds he would be hawking round the box playing
pocket billiards and inviting him to supper. Could he
hide them with impunity behind the lockers until the
happy batchelor had scowled askance?

F. observed Millie's Guinea Pig forehead and
wondered what she would be like down in the basement.

Her lips were smothered in their mother's bright red
lipstick and she was kinked in irregular high-heel
shoes.

The randy Alsatian dog which was always so ready to
mount their creamy thighs was peering over the wall at
the bottom once more. The brute hungrily sniffed for
her scent.

"Oh, please?" they begged him. "We'll do anything
you ask...Lucy will pull down her knickers or do the
washing-up." What a choice to have to make.

"I'm sorry, but you'll both have to skidaddle," said
the Flash. "I've got other fish to fry and I don't
want you coming round here any more." But the words
cracked like *shulamar* in his throat.

A fulvous flash telegraphed the arrival of the
'Signalling and Telecommunication's' van as it came
hurtling up the brow of the hill.

In moments the scouts would swing into the little
patch of wasteland, and the technicians would burst out
of the back door like the exprobrate Sweeney.

"If you don't let us come again," said Millie,
pouting her lips and resting her hand on her blossoming
hip, "then we'll go home and tell our father and mother
that you've been playing dirty games in the barn."

She sulked bad temperedly and fingered her
developing aureole.

But F. coolly called their bluff and scurried them
to the secret passage where their feet would be wrapt
in cloud.

"Go on then!" he said. "I dare you! I don't care.
They won't believe you anyway when I tell them about
your bribes."

Millie hornily reddened and scampered over the
hedge.

They danced and cavorted towards the Gents where
Malcolm had recently paused.

Lifting their schoolskirts and touching up their
quims they followed *Joe Miller* inside, then ran out
sniggering.

Millie expertly simulated the *act of copulation* at
the pillar and Lucy clumsily followed. The *philistines*
acted totally without inhibition much to F.'s delight,
and misery.

Before *Galen* clapped the lower door to check the blurb
of miter in the wallow muck F. decided to refer through
the pages of his billowing dictionary:-

Pervert: 1 Turn to wrong use 2 lead astray
(person/mind) from right opinion or conduct 3 One who
shows unhealthy abnormality especially in sexual
matters, or religious belief: wayward and self-willed!

Loitering omniverously in the doorway with his eagle
eye on the traffic below, after consuming his daily six
egg omelette, the *pervert* perlustrated 'Slack' Alice as
she made her way down the lane to school. She revealed
her hairy armpits in an effort to give him an
enthusiastic wave.
   "Hiya," she called. Her moustache was certainly
getting thicker. Alice brought him greetings from her
mother, who was having an affair with a local
councillor in the sleepy Hamlet.
   F. had to laugh at her description of the areas
occupants, who she described as the 'Flower generation
trapped in a sixties time warp.'
   The peroxide blonde invited him to her imminent
sixteenth birthday party. She could not understand his
refusal after going to the trouble of fixing him up
with *Kelly*. But the muscleman had to retire home for
his beauty kip.
   It was later in the morning that he noticed a
strange fellow stroking his dark pointed beard and
staring monotonously from the bushes over the truck of
the bilge. The visitor was dressed like a *Funeral
director*.
   Up the lane from the *ironbridge* marched a group of
fledgling schoolboys.
   Thirty of the deviant troope with dark piercing eyes
pressed into the dismal and dowdy recesses of the
Greenhouse.
   The schoolmaster asked them if they had any
questions to ask him concerning his occupation. A
conspicuous silence ensued from the *little lords of
Solomon* as they spun in confused circles.

The different race with their mouths inquisitively
agape covered the archaic walls of the cabin and
digested the special instructions near the diagram.
Their long hair distended down each precipice of their
lobes...

He gratefully shook F.'s hand before leading the
queer crew back into another dimension.

As soon as they were gone the man with tunnel vision
observed the gully for Leonora curbing quietly back
from town...she finished at noon on Wednesdays.
Sometimes she suffered from dizzy spells. But the
medical reports were always diligently performed.

Doddering up the lane and lingering by the wall she
hid from the light in the 'buck up' of capturing a
winged insect.

She journeyed up the bank to home before returning
with something more fetching in a t-cup.

As he warmly proffered her up the stairs he quickly
ran to hide the copper kettle. She placed her plate of
crackers on the training bench.

After testing the hardness of his chest the mother
of four happily consented to his request.

She unbuttoned her white shirt blouse, which was
always ironed the night before in readiness.

F. was soon smothered in her massive udders and
sucking her ratchet nipples. D-cup.

He suggested she demonstrate just how *Belinda
Swashbuckler* had primed frankfurters. He prodded her
stud with his creese.

The wench's canteen eyes filled with rabid rapture
as she stuffed the chamber of her *Little Mary*. She
began to iron out the wrinkles on his foreskin..."Look
at the size of you!" she sighed luxuriently.

"I've only ever done this with my better half," she
paled. "I suppose you think I'm just a woman of the
stews?"

Kneeling on the brown lino floor before him she
swallowed the gorgon penis whole and tried to digest
her recent scobs in the process.

"Do you like it then?" asked F. as her trunk plunged up
and down the stalk for hours.

"Not 'alf!" groaned Leonora, and made another
spirited attempt to deep throat the cornucopia en mass.
"If god made anything better, then he kept it to
himself," she choked. "Nobody swallows gum like I
can!" she ranted. The old ones are the best?

He forced the automoton powerfully down with her
hands floating and half resisting, struggling in the
void, and loaded to the gunnels.

Eventually they rested neatly on his waist but she
still gagged once more for air. The frothblower
boggled like three sheets in the wind about the sudden
swell which made her reach for the skies.

Her demented head tinged with the first onset of
grey erupted slurping and gobbling demeaningly with a
wail of spray.

Leonora forced his foreskin roughly back as she
plummeted and chaffed the sensitive sides against her
hot flooding chasm, occasionally glancing up to study
his sentinel expression. The lace meat obviously
needed a good watering of bladder oil. School
meals...yuck!

Once more she sensed the vomit rising uncontrollably
in her gizzard. The *milkmaid* apologized profusely for
her impropriety as she tried to lash the waves. He
casually cajoled her into complete submission although
her shark teeth could have snapped through timber.

The Signalman could feel the load jolting against
his throbbing erection and spasming near her gullet.

Suddenly her gulping orifice ebulliently withdrew as
she threw herself expiringly to the jib coughing like a
bulaemic. And they said that chivalry was dead.

Leonora puked her last dish over the swabdeck and
wiped her slobbering gob on his turn-ups.

She glared at him as if he had the devil to
pay..."Salmon!" she boasted. A likely story! More
like tuna chunks. There was certainly something fishy
going on at the Zoo.

With hungered flesh obscurely, she mutely craved to
adore. Was she expecting a tip?

The white faced relict stared dazed and confused around the room without knowing if she was coming or going...

"I don't know how much longer I can go on with this!" she confessed with bleary eyes ablaze. "Do you think you'll ever be able to see the sunrise?"

Once more the Locomotive approached before he could cartel. F. quickly rose to tender the number in the 'Train describer' and pull up his trousers, with Leonora still floundering like an ulcer between his balls of hay. Man's gotta do what a man's gotta do.

The driver of the 10.30 stared aghast through the open window. He seemed totally polaxed as he pulled slowly up the platform into the station.

"I don't want you to take all this too serious, do you understand," said the young man. "Please don't keep coming down here all the time pestering me, as it would interfere with my physical culture."

Leonora suddenly began blubbering. What was she going to do? When push came to shove.

Have hysterics and embarrass him by throwing a stone inside the circumvallation of the Glasshouse? Or invite him round to dine with his kit bag.

"All I want is a man around me," she murmurred sadly, her lustful eyes shining upward and suddenly becoming blurred again.

She tore off her dress and raced out of the door, threatening to jump over the shale, if he wouldn't play 'Trains and Tunnels.'

But just as the virgin was getting laid, and she screwed herself forcefully upon his protesting penis, enveloped by the encompassing darkness in the cubicle to disguise her vexing stretchmarks, the faint reverberation of six bells danced down the steps and caused his ears to prick bolt upright.

"There's much more space for your *Moby Dick* in my 'Gladstone' than this tired old gob love. I told you it would be nice in there..."

"Jesus Christ!" cried the Flash, as his angry foreskin suffered a bloody baptism.

He charged from the deep interior to helter-skelter back up to the gantry.

"You thought you were a man, but you're not!" she
hissed. Certainly scraping the barrel.

   With his kegs at half mast and struggling with his
equipment he hesitated before acknowledging the
Obstruction Danger signal.

   Slamming the relevant pegs back on and quickly
operating the emergency detonators at the crossover he
answered the phone to the Junction with one hand
covering his cod-piece.

   Cancelling the train on which the passengers lives
were at risk he stood trembling at the door with the
trousers round his ankles.

   "Are you alright mate?" Linus alertly replied.
"There's a broken rail outside the goods yard, what
have you been doing up there all day may I ask?"

71

By nightfall she was fired from the string, so he
locked the door in case she tried to sneak back while
he was recuperating, placing a sign over the
aboriginal; 'Strictly no admittance!'

At just after witching hour he extended his long
refracting telescope, before the silvermoon expired.

Weaving its magic spell before plunging the planet
once more into darkness the orb disappeared behind a
scudding shade, and did not reappear until *housel*.

In the harsh March wind the girls huddled augustly
together on the wooden bench. They trembled like
kittens as he approached to discover ways of
alleviating the tragic situation...

Camping out in only their sleeping bags on the hard
terrain the little waifs had returned down the pasture
from the mountainside, and had missed their last train
home to Pendle. But as luck would have it the P.Way
Pirates were out in force again and were smuggling
their gear along the platform to the lighted grotto.

"What on earth are you doing here at this time of
night?" asked the Signalman patter-eternally. He
coaxed them up to the warm house; when the coast was
clear he would phone for a taxi...he promised!

In the compound below Inspector Gilbert assembled
the floodlighting for the 'Engineer's Possession.'

On the gallery bank his chrome dome dazzled everyone
in·sight by its reflective glare, until they moved the
main operation to a mile distant from the points.
Without looking where he was going he tripped over a
signalling wire and fell flat on his face.

He slowly rose and made his way up to the Signalbox
to sign over the line. After entering the cabin he
dismantled his 'high visibility vest' and began to make
friendly conversation with the garrison crew ensconced.

"Poor beggars," said the Signalman, marking the prey
for his own. "Gone and missed their life-belt. I'll
run them home early in the morning."

It was easy to turn the tables on the look-out as he
lodged against the doorway in his drags.

"Well, I suppose you've got work to do now?" sighed
the Flash. The girls quickly whitewashed his decision
to depart...sorely outranked!

Lisa suddenly decided on a striptease from her blue
jeans into her short crimpolene dress. She pretended
to shelter behind her two young cohorts as they
wriggled seditiously in the corner. F. watched in
disbelief, wickedly counting all his chickens.

He spread the venison liberally around the fire
before starting a game of pontoon which they had all
played before.

"This is what we do when we get bored playing
truant," snorted Lisa...

After squirting a specimen of the *boss-stick* in her
polythene bag she placed the end over her mouth and
nose. Then she sharply purled her lungs. The
experience seemed to refrigerate her skin.

She came to sit opposite him and lifted her perfect
legs onto the side of the armchair. The girl continued
to widen her creamy white thighs.

"He's looking up your dress!" tittered Melanie, but
her friend simply moaned that she was feeling weary.

"What a little cracker!" he celebrated. "Nice big
mammaries and cast in beautiful proportion. And no
horrible stretch marks!"

Once more the tired old Inspector kicked his boot
against the cellar-rail and plodded up the stairs to
make a mashing in the *cockloft*. He signed the book to
give the *up* road back to his scheming host, and warned
him of an imminent change of P.I.C.

Inspector Gilbert repented his disturbance in
sackcloth and ashes, but asked the rogue in charge of
the *Casino* if he thought the red-headed urchin was old
enough to smoke. The old man stuttered and stodged his
way through break-time communion by farthing candle.

Lisa began applying some golden eye-shadow around her
wet blue eyes, and was looking prettier and more
gullible by the second. She poured scorn on her
boyfriends attempts to woo her after the youth-club.
'What I need is a more experienced man,' she beguiled.

"How do you fertilize a Whale?" she jested. "Send
some *seamen* down!" The unsteady Inspector choked and
left his scurvy mug half drunken.

"I want to be an 'Air Hostess' when I grow up," said
Melanie suddenly. Not another one! The 'Undertaker'
looked up at the clock and shook his head fatefully at
the crew. Flipping Zebedee!

"It's time for bed girls," fussed the slippery
Captain perseveringly. His fingers were already
touching the fastening of his common mate.

Lisa rubbed her spuming eyes and pulled a coat over
her legs to oscillate.

As the innocent waifs unrolled their tardy sleeping
bags beside the gantry a sombre *Argand* sibilated its
noxious portent in the close opaque mist above the
cobbled lane. Teach your granny to suck eggs!

The slim companion arched its Giraffe neck through
the gloom to peer curiously into the other lantern.
Its sigma was drowned out by the trumpet-toned jive and
clashing of cymbals...

On the silent earth a sublime breeze brewed and
began to rock the arches of the stern-wheeler
hypnotically from side to side...a single bulb swang
remotely from the unhinged eaves. The black silhouette
suddenly sprang across the rigging of the window stay
from the *phenomenal* world.

With Lisa's head resting pensively on the sleeve of
the armchair he shuffled to the cupboard where the
slush was stored. Salvaging his favourite fantasy he
returned to stand before her. He opened the magazine
at page one where the *Maiden* swam full of surprise with
her merit lost at sea.

His hazy vision ebbed and flowed as he swaggered
like a tipsy with the noggin.

Lynched by the yeast blowing in the gale the swooning
girl held her hand self-consciously over her mouth in
case the voyage should induce vomitting.

Rocking in the hazardous blast of the weather beaten
'Flying Fish' the swashbuckler held on tightly to his
masthead and reached for the exposed clip of her slip.

With this conjuror's rod he invoked the spirit of
somnolence and scanned the far horizon for disagreeable
encroachers. The wives of the 'buck-and-ear!' She
awoke intuitively to the sudden noise of a metal tool
being struck against the keel outside. His throbbing
penis was only inches from the ocean of drooling saliva
seeping from her western shoreline.

"Leave my fanny alone!" she hoarsely wheezed. She
turned to face the chaffing-dish from the felon baulked
of conquest. Fancied a drink of 'duck's wine!' Fine.

The Flash with the 'fire in his eye' thought he saw
a glimpse of something long since banished, 'emicating'
in the glass beneath the groaning wooden rafters, as he
embrangled in the roaring twenties fury.

Even as the fingers of frost spread their wizard
tendrils over the hard core of the rail bed the giant
miscalculation arose from the heart of darkness...

He grinned in harridan at his own reflection as it
glimmered on the bolt head and tossed the nebulous
stake of virtue, which had been ripped from his
nocturnal pulse, contemptuously across the sulphur.

Nosferatil leered haughtily at the cruising Afrite
supining so sweetly on the silver nightstage and
shrugged his shoulders arrogantly astern. He yawned
and stretched his arms towards the down-trodden meat
awaiting his hungry penis on the fawn-flecked canvas.

Gleaming like albumen in the sordid crepuscule the
crouching fiend angled slyly for his witless quarry.
The hooked nose had swelled with a distension of dropsy
but this did not prevent Grendel from dimming all the
radium to set about his job. A croaking troat of
banter humming down the basin of the escarpment made
him forever vigilant however.

His rages flexed...

With a white fanged smile he veered towards the
youngest of his escutcheon flashing his hirsute penis
and prodding the beast against her lissom prow.

As he gently lifted the brim of Vanessa's bright
shroud from her wallow the opal shimmer of a crucifix
revealed itself falling from her neck. Her harrowed
eyes opened instinctively, watching him carefully until
he had retreated to a safe distance.

Grendel motioned moodily around the hull for a
placable well-wisher who would indulge themselves in
his milk of heathen kindness.

She was sinking deeper into the coma he had woven
with his indirect influence. He checked to see if the
holy chalice was still spotless.

Millicent had a beautiful comet of long red hair
spilling over the margin of her labia. A full wide
mouth which contrasted her kite like frame was girt
with a zodiac of fresh blood.

The 'ne'er been had' stirred restlessly in her
troubled repose. Even Grendel felt a chord of pity
strike his heart when he recalled her sad necrology.

White faced love filled with the rich bouquet of
life tilted her ruby lips perfectly to forty-five
degrees and dangled her jingling arm unconsciously over
the cushion, twitching spasmodically as she mumbled
deliriously in her night dreams.

A dark shadow passed outside the contours of the
lighthouse. The figure went unnoticed as the glutton
bent ever nearer and slid his parbuckle along the
length of her labial phonograph.

Her arm jerked like a crane and a frown evaporated
across her brow as the throbbing purple of his ruddy
skin pressed ever tighter into the stolen recess of its
bay. Once more jarring against her pretty white bur
with the bloated outer vessels of his conch shell
pincered. Happy as a pig in a pea-door-file ring.

Through prunes and prisms the pedantic deviant
propelled rhythmically against her mumping hold,
supporting his cramping effort with an arm on
terrafirma, and jowling against her soft pink cheek

now and again as the gorgon thalamus hardened and free-
wheeled sideways. Her dessicated lips gradually
drifted further though he was bedevilled by the loss of
his circulation.

Her cotton lids vellicated in rapid eye movement as
the enormous forecastle of his gnarled dragon-head
began to ejaculate at her mouth's tip.

With his evil in the air he pulled away to spurt
some of its tangy juice upon her nuptual freckles. His
ecstatic groan reached to the topmost cobwebs spun
across the crowsnest even though he attempted to
suffocate his song and dance.

Great globs of grout were reservoired in the gap of
her damned puce gates and hawsered like vinculum
between her perfect molars, as the monster flew to the
cupboard to uncover his diseased 'box of tricks.'

From the fog he heard a shallow curse as the
Inspector tripped over a shovel lying in the four
foot...

He wiped the teeming ambrosia from her decaying
parts with a gospel of black tulip and mopped the drops
of reeking acid which had dripped from the tip of her
tongue onto the sole deck.

Licking his blue lips *Grendel Nosferatil* romped
across the stage, and returned rapidly back to
'normal'...

The night-mayor from *Forty-thousand fathoms* wrapped a
silken blanket lovingly round her form having
peremptorarily satiated his voracious requirement.

On the square window *lens* the atmospheric hoar frost
melted into a myriad of argent images as the refulgent
dawn modified the outer 'Hebrides' during the tolling
of the bells.

In quarter of an hour his relief would be bobbing
round the corner bang on the nail. He dawdled for
urgent seconds to deliberate.

"Come on now girls," he wailed abrasively, shaking
and stirring them from their forty winks. "It's time
to rise and shine!"

The floaters droiled with leaden eyes for anxious eons.

"Do we have to go so soon?" moaned Lisa. She clambered about the level plane to find her belongings.

The girls formed a disorderly queue before the seedy wash basin and bickered dozily.

He eventually observed their demise along the platform at a slow speed of knots with a sigh of relief!

No sooner had they turned the corner of the barrier than Bernadette appeared like a *typhoon* holding a gardening fork in one hand and a *basket of garlic* bulbs in the other.

He crusaded verbosely over harbour slabs to confirm his deep suspicions.

As the lordosis lord opened the door of the Glasshouse he stood statically in the gap. F. awaited his ducks and drakes.

"Schoolgirls?" snapped the stick insect like a sharp electric charge. He hesitated as if he were expecting an appropriate reply.

The rake grinned uncontrollably and side stepped round the obstacle.

As he passed the stationary *Pirate* bus near the entrance the Woodnymphs began to dismount down the steps. Inside the van a taciturn gaggle of whites glared in their wake.

.To his horror he noticed at once the dessicate smear across her pleasure-garden. Had there been a mutiny?

"I thought that I told you to wait at the bridge!" he complained. The girls crammed like sardines into the confined space of his Spitfire.

F. contemplated his inevitable disposal when the rumour was circulated, as it undoubtedly would, to the Signalling Inspector. A sorry scandal would effuse.

"Can we come back and visit you again in your little house?" smiled the eager housewife gazing with reverance.

"Not for the moment," frowned F. "I have a few problems to sort out first!" Not 'alf!

The girl's voracious eyes lit up like empty stars.

"I had to spit it all out into a wine glass!" she giggled.

"That's the last time I'm doing that one for a while."

"My mother wants me out of the house. Can I come and lodge with you? Do you want some *blow?*" she asked. "We can't leave it alone now."

A bluetit flew in through the open door having followed the trail of crumbs, and spent many minutes trying to escape.

He eventually threw himself against the glass in desperation and lay stunned along the cinder.

She spontaneously cupped her hands and released him into the wilderness.

With at least twenty schools to her credit *Slack Alice had* already been expelled from most of them.

Her liberal parent had initiated the smoking of dope at fourteen as they toured the countryside in a Gypsy caravan from pillar to post.

With the *utility girl* lolling in the armchair the sound of heavy footsteps sounded up the chamber. She quickly departed via the secret passage with a sloppy kiss for his supper.

The *Man in black* tapped, and entered the box at a steady rate of knots.

"Hello mate! he gleamed. "Any chance joining you in a spot of 'Pumping Iron' today? I wish I had your nerve."

"Come and sit yourself down," smiled the Flash. "Want a cup of char? Do you know that I've just been promoted to the Junction?"

The user-friendly Bodybuilding Bobby on his beat rested his long legs on the stool and described the criminal element in the village. He expressed his regret that they would no longer have an informer at the den.

F. showed him the massive black dildo with batteries
which he had found lying behind Walter's old sea-chest.
"What do you suppose that is?" he asked.

"Don't suppose you heard about the death of the
Signalman while on duty?"

F. reported the *story of Horace* who had been caught
with his pants down by the concerned train driver. He
had walked up to the Signalbox after longer than usual
stood at the stop signal to find the *Ring* of the
Signalman's penis connected by a copper wire to the
main electricity supply in the 'Block Bells and
Instruments.' A docket from *Deep throat* was still
clutched in his grasper...

The Flasher painted a horrid picture of how the
right side of the Signalman's head had melted like wax
as it rested against the three bar grill.

Suddenly his radio pipped. "It's my boss coming up
the hill!" he panicked. "He's checking up on me again
since my recent spate of Yarboroughs."

VII

THE LONELY HEARTS CLUB BAND

While pulling his plonker beneath the flickering pink tubes of the hothouse he revued his recent membership of 'Perfect Match' Introductions.

Perhaps a loving mate might still await who could sew the bonds of friendship. It was said that no matter who you were there was always someone out there just right for you. A bird of passage in search of their other half...so he placed his thumb contentedly in his mouth and continued slapping on the dish head.

He listened until Linda came in through the door and locked it behind her; true there were some hurdles to jump; for instance, not all the list appeared available to him; the seventy year old invalid; maybe the proprietor had accidentally included her data; and the housewife from the Midlands who expressly stated 'Definitely no Bald Eagles.'

One of the *Alien Nation* had obviously recognized his vital statistics from the precise description he submitted.

In a matter of days there had been a request played on Radio Caroline...'For the lonely Signalman at *Old Salem* Junction.'

He'd felt a right Charlie when it was played over the air. Since then *Ramsbottom* had been pestering him every day to pop over for some extra company, but the 'bugger-and-bum-boy' wasn't actually what he'd had in mind.

Plink plink, fizzzz...the tubes of 'Sunny's suntan centre' purled to the electric flow of the volts, and he could hear her climbing under the frame and lowering down the cover. By sundown he would be able to return to the nest...they were practically encouraged to have a healthy shower at the place of incandescence.

While the warden gathered up her magazine and retreated
to a 'safe distance' the Merry Widow peered through her
opened curtain rail.

Feigning to read her latest 'Mills and Boon' as he
stumbled from the cubicle clutching nothing but his
erection she always gave herself a good fingering while
the ugly flasher crept around the floor...

"What do you dream about when you're tanning on the
bed?"

"Nothing much," the girl sighed suspiciously
flinching on her bench.

"What do you think about when you're all alone in
yours? I usually fall asleep in mine."

When her voice had become mute F. removed the
restrainer glove from his *old man* and slithered from
his perspiring matress. Sliding over the ground he
perched like a '*praying mantis*' outside her veil. His
torso was rapidly assuming the appearance of a skinned
tomato from the long visiting hours.

Carefully prizing the curtains apart he peered
through the sly kaleidescope. Her blemishes fluttered
like a purple scarf in the phosphor and his tentacle
stirred rapidly to life.

F. removed the goggles from his beady eyes and
fastened on the apples of her Tor. His breathing must
have sounded like a pair of rusty bellows because
'Linda' suddenly turned to face him. That was the name
in the 'Appointments register' anyhow...Even the whirr
of the fan failed to mask his beat.

Only inches away from doom F.'s heart thundered over
the bumps like an out-of-control 'steam-roller.' When
at last she replaced her guard the deviant was able to
ejaculate in tenths of a second.

He was still loitering when she emerged fully
dressed from her compartment..."Fancy going out to the
gym sometime?" Had to be a first time for everything.

"Haven't I seen you somewhere before?" she replied.
With dismay F. recognized her as the *missie on the
swings*...it was years since he had exposed himself from
the limen of *Harold Park Bogs.*

The gentle Flash awoke in the early hours to a horrible
nightmare; huge brown rodents were nourishing their
ravenous appetite in the derelict basement of *Kirke*.

His Cowboy boot plunged through the rotten
floorboards only to be gnawed by their roaring chain
saw.

Her advert had read :-

'Warm and 'loving Libran.' Attractive, kind,
thoughtful, extremely sensitive and vulnerable.
Occupation: district nurse. Fond of animals.
Penthouse and landaulette, but feels that life has lost
its sparkle. Interested in Astrology and the Fine
arts. Owns two terrapins, six goldfish (two of whom
are named 'Lancelot and Percival') and a Siamese cat
called Merlin. Age 31. Seeks sincere and gallant
Knight in shining armour to fill that empty space and
sweep me off my feet!'

She sounded interesting, but it was after midnight when
he picked up the Candlestick phone to hear her faint
sounding mewl...

Her letter of eight pages length had been written in
red ink and the mathos of the *Brothers Grimm.*

"I'm so sorry darling," she sobbed. "But I was
delayed for extra duties in Cardiology. Did you like
the photographs of me on duty in my nurses outfit. I
had them taken especially for you darling."

He agreed that she looked very sexy. There was
something about black nylons and suspender belts. The
dresser chuckled soothingly to him during three hours
of sweet nothings...

"When am I going to meet you darling? What big
muscles you have," she sawdered. "There's no need to
be shy of little me."

His foot was squeezed in a vice.
All she wanted was a bit of 'T.L.C.!'

Things were certainly looking up.
"When am I going to meet you?"

Then just as suddenly her whole nature changed to
black.

His heart beat like a thundercrack but still he went
ahead with their meeting in the concrete tower.

She was said to reside in an area of unsurpassed
opulence yet the children playing on the streets seemed
unable to raise the wind.

"I'll ring before you set off darling. Just so you
don't get cold feet and to see that you are safely on
your way..."

When he spoke to her on the intercom she sounded
like a completely different person.

"Hello, it's me!" he annouced in a warm and friendly
vein...her chords maliced brumal and out-of-range. She
gave him the impression there was a secret onlooker.
But it really must have been the product of his own
shadow. He simulated flies with seventy-pound
dumbells. The naive flasher?

"Can I come in?" If he didn't like her he could
always leave...the heavy lich-gate crumbled open and he
entered the icy atmosphere of a muffled drum.

The woman answered the decorated door in a most
strange manner. She would not in any way look directly
at him. Was he really so bright? She later informed
him this was due to her shock at seeing his appearance.
He handed over the gift of 'After eight' mints. She
rustled up a Garribaldi...

"You're not at all like the image you paint," she
explained to him.

Janis wore a short white blouse, uncovering her
midrift, and a slick pair of bellbottom jeans.

Mounted on her stumpy fingers were the baubles of
glass which she said had been showered on her by the
rich businessmen of an archipelago. She was accustomed
to a life of solvency it seemed...her hanging abdomen
was littered with a *Nile delta* of albescent metal.

The *Flash* could not help staring at her maze of
ravelled white as he followed along the route through
the embellished hall.

Whoever heard of a pint-sized bouncer! In-deed/

Even the *cabin-de-thunder* walls of her ninth floor flat
were covered with a wyrd tapestry of stickers...the
cubicle served as a storehouse of condoms. He felt
transported into an underworld of distorted mirrors
larger than the inner *Tardis*.

Tokens of magic and mysticism mixed with holy
missals dripped among the bookshelves. She professed
to have been brought up a good little Catholic girl and
'always' went to holy mass on Sundays. A copy of the
good book nestled as a door-jam in support of this
claim.

Elaborately designed wallpaper in maverick gore and
gold covered every crevice of the dissolute chamber.
Above the fireplace, reflecting her obsessive tendency,
perched her mounted display of rare 'Butterflies.'
Videos in every room added to the speculation he might
be in a depository. 'Dorsement from the *Dark
Continent*,' she said. A three-foot-six high bust of
'Thoth' suddenly caught his eye, hovering erect on the
anvil. Her japan sofa was extravagantly gilded with
glittering moonstone.

"I want you to name the rest of my goldfish for me,"
she said. "I don't know any more Arthurian names
myself and you're something of an expert I believe.
You are very lucky being invited here," she told him.
"Not even my most substantial totum has been invited
into my own home."

She threw herself on the floor at his feet and
poured him a generous helping of Campari, pointing
expressly to the Crystal Chandelier which tinkled above
the *Persian rug*. Some of the lasses at the Infirmary
had bought it for her when she had been leaving...*der
Uraeus* hung in its cabinet.

On the mantelpiece was a picture of her 'piebald,'
which seemed very like an old travellers. She showed
him a photograph of when she pirouetted through the
principalities of the masquerade. Janis now tutored at
the local University on the subject of *Precious
metals*...she'd certainly made a 'fast buck' somewhere!

From closer in he could now see the worn wrinkles of
her aged rind. Though he could not perceive a single
neutral tint on her immaculate black scalp she could
have been a crone underneath all the duplicitous craft.
Her malachite eyes met his...Flash was intimidated by
their intenseness and the depth of power which he had
never before witnessed.

She offered him a professional business card. The
mistake in her qualifications had been a printing
error.

Suddenly the door of her bedroom was pushed open by
an unseen visitor, and in a flash there stood before
him the woad coloured shape-shifter called Merlin.

As if to question the identity of the stranger
Merlin turned to her and made a mannish utterance. The
swashbuckler fell increasingly under the sluggish spell
of the setting while the cat drank in his every word
and vetted him.

Each time the woman devoted her attention to her
date Merlin reacted jealously as if it were part human
and snarled up at the intruder occupying his place of
prominence. He crept along the length of her back and
over her shoulder to lean across and kiss *Krystle*
triumphantly on her mouth.

Merlin's radiant eyes imbued their spooky *guanine*
and smirked remorselessly at him. F. vitrified like a
block of marble and withdrew his contact.

She patted him lovingly. "Don't be like that
Merlin," she cajoled him.

"He's a friend; it's alright. I want you to be his
friend," she instructed the vagabondage. The cat
nodded stubbornly at her request.

Merlin glared deploringly as she lounged at the
hero's feet. He suddenly made a dash across the hearth
on which he stood guard, but the woman castigated him
instantly.

"That's very bad of you!" she said. "You'll have to
go outside."

The control protested vehemently as she led him away
to the stars.

He continued to bay the moon like a child who had been
sent early to bye-byes.

"When in doubt, leave it out!" she said. "What you
see is what you get!" she said. "Mean what you say,
and say what you mean."

As he approached her chasm she pretended to close
her eyes in repugnance. Then she immediately began
french kissing him with such ferocity that F. was
unable to understand her reaction when he reached to
touch her gland.

Her previous warmth was gone and below him lay an
angered Amazon.

Her cold and ruthless eyes petrified him with the
Gaze of the Gorgon. She suddenly burst into tears and
said he had better think about vacating the premises.
That she was not that sort of woman. Her erratic
behaviour became increasingly alarming!

Any sensible person would have departed quickly from
the scene but F. tried to calm her down and soldier to
the bottom of the mystery. After he apologized she
once again began responding passionately.

On repeating his previous apparent blunder the woman
pulled away with warlike force. Her reaction this time
was extra threatening. For one awful moment F. thought
that she would hit the roof but her temperament
gradually subsided into woe. He grinned!

In a glacier of tears she attempted to construct the
slings and arrows of outrageous fortune which had
dissipated her calamitous journey through *Archeus.*

He actually lent her his handkerchief which made the
woman smile...sitting on a stool of repentance and
recanting his profiteering.

"I'm still an unadulterated maiden," she howled.
"No-one one will ever love a fallen woman! My marriage
was never consumated because my husband turned out to
be gay."

"But didn't you find that out before you married
him?" queried the greenhorn.

She carried on with the tale which faded into
loom...

"He slashed me with a coulter when I arrived back at
the hatch and found him in the shower with my brother!"
she wept. Real tears streamed over her powdered cheeks
and rolled down her oblivious neck. Her feline probe
filled with making poison and her menacing prowled
onward.

"I feel as if I've let the grass grow underneath my
feet," she grieved. "Sitting on my tod by the fireside
every night like Cinderella," she fretted. "I've
almost resorted to put on my best hat and coat to find
some masculine company in the *Red light* district. Why
is it that every time I go into a bar the punters make
a B-line?"

A *February odour* lurked beneath her warm exterior
occasionally resurrecting itself behind the facade, and
stealing into the living room as they spoke...they laid
out the word game upon the stone table.

As they settled down to play F. became increasingly
frustrated and irritated by her diabolic machination
with numbers. In no time at all she had accumulated a
score of over four hundred points. If he disputed her
spelling she needled that he was only green with envy.

His first encounter confided that her powers of
observation and insight were directly descended from
her predecessor, who had suddenly put in an covin
appearance at his side.

She subtly gnawed at his crumbling concentration
while whispering to her invisible grandmother that he
was a simple countryman. Apart from a slight tingling
sensation F. felt fine...it came as quite a relief to
hear from her lips that the grandmother was not a
malevolent spirit. Her foglamps nodded sublimely in
her supposed direction.

In the winter-bound plateau the Tom let out a blood
curdling yell to remind them of his absence on the
balcony. Till hell freezes over!

Janis said that on no account was she allowed to
utter her 'Magisters'' dub.' F. would not be able to
defend himself with his muscles against 'that' presence
if it keenly manifested itself.

Suddenly the slate beast sordined. A rat-tat-tat
issued from the bedroom wall nearby. F. asked if they
were the only mourners in the mausoleum but the woman
remained antipodean.

She confided that after her unhappy annullment she
had changed her name to prevent her ex-husband from
discovering her whereabouts. She shivered as she
anguished about the past. It was impossible to obtain
a rational explanation, although the media seemed to
have been involved in her detective work at a
particular moment.

Hopelessly pursued by folly he persuaded her to give
him a demonstration. The savant juggled her bare feet
on the carpet and shuffled nervously as if irritated by
the wool pile...

"You have a vacuum cleaner in the boot of your
Spitfire!" she sternly enunciated.

F. gasped with surprise. How did she know that?
"I can see your Pa-Pa," she smiled with her eyes
tightly shut. "He has very small feet for his height;
size six I guess..."

Right again! He couldn't remember vaguely
mentioning...

"I don't like your sister!" she pressed. "She's a
spoilt little bitch...do you want me to have a look in
my crystal ball for you, or read the Tarot. Although
I'm afraid it will be like looking at my fetch."

"Can you see anything at all in the future?" he
asked "What are my prospects? F. noticed how she kept
glancing oddly into space.

The daughter of the hell-cat turned her attention on
him and concentrated her tiger intent, becoming more
animated as she described his haven, and wincing when
she saw the *presence* she was sure infested the retreat.

"Prepare yourelf for a shock," she resumed. "This
haunting will get much worse. Have you heard anything
at night yet? You will, mark my words!" He still had
to drive through the dead of night. She took him by
storm.

"Are you certain of your facts?" he asked. A cold
finger seemed to scratch down his spine and he gulped
to bridge his scepticism.

"It's the vile revived corpse of a fallen angel,"
she confirmed.

"Somebody you've crossed swords with the day before
yesterday...and you're going to sell your useless
sportscar to buy me an engagement ring," she added.

F. was downtrodden by a stampede of spectral horses.
Even Hammer horror films made him sleep with the lights
on. He tried to be objective and explain it by means
of her suspect mentality. The glass goblets in her
cabinet shivered like a house of cards.

"What do you see when you look at me?" he asked
pensively, trying to change the point of emphasis.

She fastened her coven eyes directly on the trapped
animal soul of the *Wickerman*..."First there's wood,
then there's paper, then there's stone!" she fizzed.

Suddenly she froze and spun away.
"Don't!" she said. "Don't look at me!" Dropping her
gaze to the limit.

A prior personage had commanded her to avaunt.
"His face is like *the King of the Jungle*!" she
imparted. "He crouches with his right hand upon your
shoulder and his growls chill me to the very bone."

"That's my ascending sign," he paled. "Can you tell
me more?"

She shook her head. "It's a ghastly breed. I cannot
look!" she confessed.

"Tell it to go away or I cannot continue." A
strange half smile rewarded on her summit.

A tremendous boom screamed from within the very
brick of her tabernacle. It sounded like the clanging
of heating pipes. Ultra-violent.

"What the hell was that?" quivered the *Flash*. The
sound nearly made him jump out of his skin. His eyes
began watering and his pulse rate quickened. He felt
himself shaking and sweat was pouring down his
emaciated mane. Offered him a black coffee.

"It's the drunk in the flat below coming in," she
calmly insisted. But F. wasn't totally convinced.
   "I know grandmother," she kowtowed, glaring where
the pentacle appeared completely desolate. "He's all
talk and not enough action...I'll tell him to go now
shall I?"
   When he examined the card again her double-barrelled
name had completely vanished.

Letters of undying love...key rings, jewellery guides,
and momentos...memorabilia. Late night telephone calls
steeped to the lips in misery. Romantic poems written
in French and smothered in kisses arrived through the
post box every single morning. Medallions, moon-rocks
of a shining white metal...
   A postcard with a 'raincoat man' exposing himself to
two delighted and impressed females, had she seen that
as well?

   To my honeybunch; the 'Flasher' - Love Tinkerbell.

And a new phenomenon arrived on the scene to confuse
matters; La 'Papillon!'
   The operative conceived she had delivered the child
on the rung. Could she have been the decoy to thimble-
rig the *apprentice*?
   She began to place the receiver in the hands of her
young charge to occupy him while she hoovered.
   The *gynander* soon began to spend more time with him
than the *Witch-Queen* herself.
   "'I love you.' When can I come for a ride in your
pap-pap?" the girl induced. F. had the definite
sensation he was being peeled. Her words seemed chosen
specially from a film score...
   She began to cry on cue and deny all
knowledge...then the *figure-flinger* would seem to
return from another portion of her web...reacting with
a sense of outrage for his doubting the sincerity of an
'innocent.'
   "Always remember," she stoked. "Emeralds are
forever, the colour of her eyes!"...

A queer despair entered her straying eyes and they
clouded into a peculiar hue of dun. The child leaned
over to admire the map on his knee and slipped her hand
over his. It was all down to him. Good job he had not
missed taking his ginseng...

Even on her *bromide images* it was difficult to
discern her true racial mix. Janis described her as
having the face of a *little China doll*. Her 'sister's'
child..."Well, we all make mistakes!" she vituperated.
'And there's nothing wrong with worshipping at the
Golden Temple.'

She was just returning from having her shooting-
brake serviced; the grey *Mercedes* pulled up alongside
in the parking lot.

In the rear window was a picture of the Madonna, and
a sign saying 'State registered nurse!' As she bent
down and looked in the passenger seat her teeth seemed
totally fossilized.

Apparently they had been witness to an unfortunate
accident. The little boy's blood had spattered over
her dress as she attended the pile-up and would not
wash away. She certainly appeared apprehensive to
return to the *Killing Fields* later on that day.

She expostulated the sackfulls of mail she was still
receiving every morning, even though she had told them
to cancel her membership. "And why haven't you?" she
fired on all four cylinders, "I rang the agency to
check!"

The flunkey tossed him a snapshot of the opposition.
The lonely batchelor's letter detailed every corner of
his apathetic bedroom.

Jandice complained his engine was in need of urgent
maintenance. In the rush she had even forgotten her
uraemia tablets.

When they arrived in the busy market street the
Castle stores were filled with ordinary weekend
shoppers. The woman who was with him expressly
mentioned that 'La Papillon' was now wearing one of her
own creations. F. could not help noticing their amused
expressions as they browsed up her short gray
miniskirt.

Emerging from a souvenir shop La 'Papillon' suddenly
presented the merchandise to her dry-nurse.   A huge
hyaline waverer with wings of sheer silk stalled in the
palm of her grab.

Janis coolly chastised the girl after he had drawn
attention to the apostle's act. What she said next
made him cherish scruples.

"Don't forget my Tarot pack!" she snarled. La
'Papillon' suddenly became very serious and dreamlike.
"She's just started her periods," whispered Janis..."We
must not be too adamant."

The closer they approached to the city the more the
woman became anxious and afraid. "I've kept away from
here for years," she maugered nervously. "Ever since
'he' was on the lurk..."

F. returned from the take-away with food for them
both to find his private drawer had been ransacked of
all its spare copper. The pair of them had piled it up
on the table and were sharing out the dividends
equally. F. was flabbergasted at their audacity.

"I didn't think you'd mind just a few pennies," she
said. "What a solitary scrooge you are."

The gynander boshed in *Siberian* double-talk. 'Can
she give you a small peck?' she wondered. "I promised
you would be dead keen."

La 'Papillon' rushed forward and kissed the Flasher
fully on his lips...there was a sweet taste; she had
put her tongue in his mouth. His expression turned a
white cream of soda.

"Oh! I'd better leave you two alone," convened the
mid-wife. She acted more as matchmaker than anything
else. Whatever your sins you'll fit right in!

F. regretted the pupil's high eastern cheekbones and
eager custom. Something was amiss. He rebuked the
shapeshifter for trying to deviate them from their
original pact.

When they had finished the 'Chinese' he uncovered
the 'I' Ching Oracle. Nothing she said seemed to speak
by the card. Although resenting the *alien dimension*
she carelessly threw the Yarrow stalks...

Janis asked if there would there be a fruitful outcome
to their union.

The Oracle replied with terrible accuracy; she would
'fall into a bottomless pit for all eternity'...the
woman reacted with an incantation of her own.

Was 'La Papillon' chimera, or simply masquerading as
one of the 'lost tribe?' He rightly guessed the awful
truth; her soul was *black* and her motives riddled with
devious corruption.

The opponent suddenly decided on a rip-tide of
watershoot. Unzipping her nylon she deliberately left
the door open and pulled the coy Flasher inside. Janis
flung the shower curtain wide attempting to expose him
to the buck private.

"Look at her face!" urged the conspirator. "She
has an inkling what we are doing." But F. refused to
give them ammunition...Were they all going up the wall?

With the lighting turned down the misbegotten crump
hid in the dead of night while they cavorted together
on the mish-mash.

Janis *Littlewhite* guided his mawler into the wide
recesses of her honeypot. It was certainly similar to
a 'paper-hanger's bucket...' but 'her' cunt had molars.

He stood over the woman's head, but she resisted.
Becoming angry when he pushed her demonstratively on
him, and refused to do him homage.

"What do you think I am?" she asked. "Why don't you
grease the palm of a call-girl if that is all you
want."

She rammed him into her prurient frame stripped to
the bone just as the next door neighbour arrived in the
corridoor to fiddle with his clavis.

"Please don't rend me by inches!" she screamed at
the top of her voice..."You must tell me how much you
love me!" And like an idiot he did. Her multiple
orgasm flowed around him like a scalding flow of lava.
She bucked like a livewire.

"Do you always have this effect on women?" she asked
him.

Her entrance flung him a lifebelt. Unmoored at the
helm his dingey floundered lost at sea.

The frightened penis felt like a skinny matchstick
stalk inside her *epileptic* cylinder but F. made a last
desperate effort to please her. He effected a good
imitation of Ram Raj.

Suddenly the skeleton at the feast threw on the
overhead beam. She stood there motionless near the
food cartons. Her pale and horrid disposition
suggested she had been devouring the flesh from
carrion. Was she in truth invaded by a *dybbuk?*

F. gazed down with disgust at those fruit on the
vine he had been so willing to pick. The old crone's
puckered waistline ridged with the canals of white heat
filled him with a feeling of absolute loathing. Her
thighs were whitewashed with cellulite.

Flash placed his hand over his pabulum tube. He
just wanted her out of his sight as soon as possible.
The *charlatan* seemed grim as an undertaker. He farted
furtively. Kept a firm hand on the tiller.

Her breastplates were lined with a redoubt. The
devil's sword had left a dyke of studded scimitar. She
reached to cover up her unfortunate scars and insisted
they were the imprints from her *breast implants...* most
irregular!

About the nether region of her loins were the
abstract zig-zag lines of her scarlet skinned attack.
The tell-tale escutcheon of *the Mad pandemic Sorcerer!*

When he closed his eyes her bust drilled its graven
image into his *unbidden* like an atomic time-piece.

All hell seemed to break lose...
La 'Papillon' wailed that she had been taken for a
ride. The squelch of a fisherman's wellies.

F. stubbornly refused to donate the pictorial
equivalent as a recompense.

They bolted from the door to hike twenty miles back
to the tower block at nearly two in the morning...

Janet parked her buggie alongside after driving all the
way down from Kirkwall to attend her helper's
betrothal.

She brought with her a lucky mascot and bannock from
the scab.

The regular nurse seemed a tolerable ray of comfort
and seemed happy to crash at the 'Flashers' overnight
with no strings attached.

When he returned after sunrise she appeared to have
had a bust up.

The phone had been ringing at regular intervals all
night but thank god she had resisted the temptation to
lift the receiver. She did not feel in the slightest
bit peckish.

When he kissed her goodbye at the bub the large
cumbersome matron adjusted her bleak brown gigs. She
seemed concerned that he would need a lightning rod
down the bolt-hole.

As the telephone rang Janet warned him to be extra
vigilant. Just as suddenly the dial went dead. He
hugged her as a matter of politeness.

She handed him a card with a baby elephant dancing
on the cover. It said, 'Remember, elephants never
forget, and I won't forget you in a hurry!' which he
thought was rather touching...

He arrived at the 'Witch's den' on the surprise
visit at four o-clock in the afternoon just when most
people were clocking off.

When she eventually let him in F. was introduced to
the two men sitting watching live television in the
kitchen. He first mistook them for *Tweedledum and
Tweedledee* from the 'Big House on the Hill.'

At the dinner table was a *salt and peppered* mental
patient in his mid-thirties who she introduced as her
half-brother, a compulsive suicide case. The other was
bodeful and forbidding; a six foot four biker in black
leathers who scrutinized the shifter in a very
questioning manner, and whose buttons fastened at the
back.

He stood up and shook F.'s hand with the confidence
that came from being the warden. Then she led him
sweeping into the living room fretting like a broody
hen. Felt like a worm in a shit pen.

Still concealed in her nightgown she appeared about to
enter one of her trancelike states of paranoic anger.
Her skin was covered in a sheen of ancient slime and
her mind seemed unable to extrapolate.

"You'd better keep talking!" she sirened. "If you
don't they'll think something is wrong. Hold me in
your arms darling," she solicited. "Put your hand to
baby. Feel him kick inside me..."

In the cold light of day F. began to panic and
ponder avenues of escape. His only chance seemed to
pacify her. He firmly promised to give her a ring as
soon as he returned home.

With a spellbound thorn on her face the woman led
him to the door doubting his honesty and disparaging
any sense of betrayal.

"Promise?" she glared.
"I give you my firm undertaking!" whittled the Flash.
His lips were motioning like mute padlock.

She gave him her *Medusa* look...he shivered in a
mortal spunk.

A dangerous partition shot across the menace of her
mood but he broke free from the pinfold and shut it
hastily behind him without a moment to lose. Janis
could have got the wind up anyone. He temporarily lost
his train of thought.

Foregoing the lift he urgently stumbled down the
outer spiral. Must have been on a promise.

At any second the werefolk would be hot on his
heels.

As he deserted the caillach in her gloaming kingdom
he felt a healthy flush arriving on his cheeks.

A host of desperate phone calls rapidly followed.
More photographs of La 'Papillon' in her swimming
costume. Christian artifacts, Crocadile tears.

"Tell me the truth?" he said. "Who are you? What
are you?"

But the woman seemed the very paragon of lies.
"Darling, oh my darling!" she sobbed in her *Fiesta*.
Jàmié a jamais... You'll always be my heartsblood..."
Dressed up to the nines in black stockings and ball
gown.

Then just as quickly the woman changed her tack and a
juice of spiteful venom issued viciously from her
smoke-screen! Her mirror shattered into a million
fragments.

"If you had faced up to your responsibilities the
Solicitor would not be required. Since I no longer
want to have 'our' child I will settle for a large
cheque to cover my abortion expenses." She assured him
that it had not been necessary to 'shoot his load.'

F. assembled every last one of her *substratum* and
reached for the *portfire*.

He sent her one last postcard; 'Tu oublieras aussi
l' eclair,' and rang the dating agency to investigate
her substance.

After checking the files back five years the
Proprietor returned rather annoyed.

"Yes! We've come across this strange customer
before!" she admitted. She'd been known by many
aliases since her fly into orbit.

"We had a similar complaint many moons ago when her
moniker was *Lilith.*"

Next in procession came the Lloyds underwriter with a
degree in Psychology. At last here was a 'lady' he
could really do business with.

"When she's sorted you out, then send her down here
to sort me out too!" cackled Jelly-degenerate on the
blower.

"Of course I've got a pretty face," she avouched.
Ever the incurable optimist F. watched her dismount
from the 'E' type with rising reluctance and stand
below him ringing the door bell.

Her locks were domed in a great ball of fuzz and her
low cut dress was shot through with stripes.

"How the hell did she get pretty out of that," he
sibilated. But her information proved to be correct in
one aspect at least.

As she bent to examine the name disc her enormous
cleavage spilled like a sugar-plum over the brim of her
party frock.

It would be a shame to turn down good food and the
woman had suddenly peered up.

The top-heavy-*Taurean* with the thin masculine lips
ambled slow and tentatively up the stairs after him.
How on earth could she refuse him with face like that?
He began to count his sure fire blessings. He'd soon
show her a clean pair of heels.

When she'd warmed up on the *cocktail of lethal
substances* after the evening meal F. was glad to find
her a source of stimulating conversation.

Appearing tense and empirical before the soup she
gradually unwound to expose an easy going temperament.
She confided in him her deep reservations at taking
such a leap in the dark.

"My mum's looking after little Lucy for me tonight,"
she said. "That's because I don't know what time I
will be back."

"Met any weird and wonderful characters yet?" he
asked. He was put under gas while she told him about
the Gad-fly bloke from Pie.

"Oho! One of those," he gasped. "I've had some
rather traumatic experiences myself. What do you
think?"

"I'm sure she's put a hex on me because every time I
meet her in my imagination it's in a *stone white
Golgotha.*"

As he described the encounters with his *night
visitor* the room turned isochemial. The rather pensive
female began to choke and tears welled in her rugged
buds. Biggest mammaries of any living mammal.

"That's almost hand in glove," she quaked. "Only
the other day when I was posting my reply the package
burst into flames."

She squeezed closer into his arms.
"Is it okay if I stop the whole night?" she flushed.
"I can't bear the prospect of sleeping alone in the
cottage. I hope you don't think that I'm a tart or
anything...this has only ever happened at the hop."

But once again the same chronic loss of appetite
reared it behemoth head, and though the single divorcee

laboured long and hard around his flacid stem, his eyes
were larger than his stomach.

The soft point of her tongue slurped along his
perineum.

What the hell did she think she was doing?
She suddenly shot her warm serpentine to his hole and
rammed her rabbit up his shit-pipe...for a beached
whale she had quite a water-spout.

While Queen B. faked slumber she was able to shake
hands with *the Bishop*.

Just as the awry bag of spanners grounded on the
Stygian shoreline his ingredients gushed like a
fountain.

She turned over a new leaf, moaned and rolled out of
his life...like a ship that passed in the night.

As he bade her valediction at the fire door in the
harsh light of dawn she buzzed..."I bet you say...'I'll
give you a ring sometime.'"

"I'll give you a buzz one of these days," confirmed
F. as treacle-chops hedge-hopped toward the hopper.

§   §   §

'WHEN IN DOUBT, GET IT OUT!' snapped F.

The staff nurse laughed out loud at the dreamer.
"I think that I know who you mean," she chuckled.
"Hold the line while I go and check the common room..."

It sounded as if he'd rang through to a conference centre. Had he been given her work number? A male voice whispered 'hello' and then vanished. Did she reside near the mouth of *Alum pot*?

Our hero eventually agreed to meet her on the platform of the station at seven o-clock that summer evening. She did acoustic tetchy and indifferent but F. put this down to first night nerves.

Travelling to the rural village stop on the train he imagined meeting someone extra special. The guard did not bother to check his credentials since he was already so famous in those parts.

'Age thirty-one. Dark hair, no glasses. Fond of reading, the countryside, and cycling. A clerk at the central branch of the city's Building Society. Absolutely stable.'

F. dismounted from the carriage and slammed the door shut. He waved goodbye to his associate and scouted round for Paula. Where could she be...sitting on the steps watching him? The platform was deserted. Would she match up to his great expectations?

He suddenly noticed someone coming towards him from the side entrance. Surely it was *homunculus* dressed in a severe *chessboard* suit with turn-ups, and looking for all the world like, yes like, *Jimmy Clitheroe!*

With a cigar in her top pocket the tiny breasted woman jockeyed over the crumbling paving stones in her loud stilleto heels resounding like a pair of kettle drums.

She curtly offered to escort him to the Hotel on the horizon where she was staying temporarily until something better could be arranged.

"Where are you're digs?" he asked.   "Do you share with
students (of life)?"   But she didn't bat an eyelid.

As they marched into the great unknown her manner
was cold and complacent.   Was she luring him to a bow-
stringing?   The cavern of cedars formed a parasol above
their heads along the lane.   The croft was curiously
inconspicuous.

"I can't stop out too late tonight," she insisted,
"but perhaps tomorrow if I ask them.   I have to be in
by nine.   House rules I'm afraid.   We could have gone
down to the Red Lion for a drink, but most of the
residents go in there. You may come back to my room for
a chat if you like.   I'll explain everything in
privacy."

As they accelerated up the winding pathway of the
spacious grounds the little gangster scuttled along the
septic tank of bedlamites.   *A laughing Cavalier* jumped
out of the bushes.

She ordered F. not to look at him...
When they dismounted from the lift one of the other
occupants was having a terrible row with her mother in
the corridoor. The *fat girl* had flung herself on the
floor and wrapped around her shins.   She slavered and
snapped at her parents ankles.   Apparently her
behaviour was identical each quarter.

The sullen six stone midget very kindly pulled a
curtain across her miserable allocation of space.
After removing her *Al Capone* she settled on her joy-
trap.   The jig-saw puzzle of the *Tower of* Babblestill
lay *jumbled on her quilt*.   On the cabinet were
photographs of her pretty young sister's recent
engagement.   Here indeed were the last incipients of
regal *Atlantis*.

Had she just swallowed her dose of *cod liver oil*?
Jimmy Clitheroe expounded that after many bad
experieces she had finally taken an overdose of
barbiturates.   Her husband had left her for his
business partner, another public school boy.   She would
never trust another man again.   What if they searched
'him' and asked for proof?

102

"It was decided that I should go on living *under
supervision* inthemeantime...I'll soon be allowed home
for the weekends," she sullenly stated. "Unfortunately
that's when the trouble usually starts. I never want
any children," she admitted. "This world is far too
wicked and unstable."

"Don't they say anything to you at work?" he naively
conferred. "Aren't you afraid of getting like any of
them in here. What about your sick leave?"

Just as she seemed about to melt there was a
terrible din in the concourse at the end of the female
dormitories.

The 'Riddler' from the grounds had followed them up
the stairs and was masturbating in full view of the
reception. F. could discern the patter of rushing feet
and a rumpus at the exit.

Jimmy grew noticeably more brumal. His two-tone
sounded terse and his treatment coiled like a knot.
The little fella' edged away from the offender blushing
on the brim of his shovel.

"You'd better go now and don't ever come back!" he
bitterly snapped. "I thought it could work but it
can't." Anymore of this and he'd be getting a, what is
it? – 'Chip on his shoulder.'

But Vivienne had been there from their *Genesis*!

He'd seen her gardening with *Blackbeard* or squatting
down at the bird table with her playthings. Then there
had been one. Where had *Blackbeard* gone? She seemed
to be blown along like a delitescent piece of string,
and she even sunbathed alone on bank holidays.

He daringly scribbled her a note:

'Dear 'Vivienne' (found on the 'Electoral Register'),

I've fancied you for ages so how about giving me a ring
sometime?'

It was 'her' next door neighbour who rang the non-
starter initially.

"Surely no sensible person sends love messages to a
perfect stranger," she disparaged. "What number do you
live at? How did you find my address?"

After some wrangling on the phone she agreed to come
straight across and introduce herself. From the
atalaya window he observed her slim figure approach.
Hurray! Vivienne seemed absolutely *normal*. He could
almost imagine a scattering of clouds?

She was wearing a loose fitting pair of hot pants
and her freckled thighs were faultless! They could
squeeze the life out of him any time of day. She
seemed like a welcome spark of sunshine...

He poured the High school gymnast a chilled glass of
dry white wine as she scorched around the wall of
amateur prints.

"You really must make an exhibition of yourself,"
she muttered. "I saw you once at the supermarket."
She'd smiled...or had he concocted that as well?

"Don't you have any friends of your own?" she asked.
"It's a very unsociable job," flushed the irrepressible
Flash.

He was hardly able to keep his eyes from her bare
legs...to think that he thought she was so shy, sweet,
and innocent.

"Why wouldn't you describe yourself on the phone?"
she nattered. What, and tell her that he looked like
the *Bald Eagle*...no chance!

The bubbly blonde from the East-end opened her full
wide mouth to display for him her silver fillings. He
peered curiously toward the cavity ready to climb
inside. This wasn't what he'd bargained for at all and
she was certainly no *vestal* 'virgin.'

"I was a bit worried at first," she admitted. "Why
don't we go out for a drink this weekend. I've been
feeling rather lonely since I split up with my
boyfriend."

Curiously enough *Ryan Starbuck* called on the blower
while she was his guest.

104

He invited F. to his Christmas shin-dig. Ryan refused
to believe the twenty-five year old woman sounded older
than any one of her pupils. Once again the *Flash* was
unavailable. The *Glassbox* would be open during the
entire extent of that ensuing leisure period.

After placing down the hand-set F. decided to make a
half-hearted pass at the visitor as she looked at his
wall drawings. She turned away. Showed him her cheek.

But he was jubilant when he saw her to the door. He
wished her goodnight and apologized for his ebullient
behaviour. "See you Saturday then," he grinned.

All night long he tossed and turned. That was a bit
early for the postman. He bolted down to collect his
mail.

Dear Misinformed (the note read),

After last night's meeting I have been thinking ahead,
and wish to cancel Saturday's dates. I think it is you
who has the wrong impression about me. I feel you want
more from me than I am prepared to give. The only
reason I came round last night was through sheer
curiosity. I like making friends, and to know people
on the estate.

I wish to make it very clear that under no
circumstances do I fancy you or want to go out with
you. I don't like people making passes at me when I
have only just met them.

Please keep your distance!
Thanks,
Vivienne.

F. screwed up the letter and threw it in the bin...

Averse to admit defeat the lion hearted fire-eater
decided to depart once more over the rampart top and
enter the stockade.

The late night 'Lonely Hearts Club' on the local radio
station provided the focus of his solace.

A young lady advertising on the channel sounded a
real belter. So he pencilled his telegram and posted
the abededary immediately to *the Pulse* with his fingers
crossed. Knew what she'd be like before he clapped
eyes on her.

With eager anticipation he dawdled at the crossroads
of the Mailcoach...a girl in cream coloured cloth and
brown slacks stepped from the trochilic dromedary.

He loitered around to obtain a closer inspection
before revealing his true identity. She was wearing a
sick 'Carnation' in her button-hole.

"Oh Yesss! I'm good looking! All my family agree
about that." A perfect candidate for the looney-bin...

She'd placed her mother on the public telephone to
vouch for her honesty and to assess his integrity and
uprightness. It did not seem appropriate at that
moment to conduct an 'obscene phone call' he thought.

Along the road she lathed and shanked the Zebra
crossing. She patrolled along the deserted patch of
scrub beside the Co-Op wall while he hid in the bus
shelter opposite. He turned his back as her crazy eyes
fastened on the only other inhabitant. The female form
began to travel slowly in his direction.

With vocal chords screeching full of desperation the
Elephant girl cornered him against the watch-glass.
She even asked if 'he' knew anyone of that
abbreviation. He hastily denied it of course and said
he was a complete stranger to the area.

She carried along the pavement bellowing his name at
the top of her voice, and becoming more frenzied and
bewildered by the second.

The sickly nuthouse pustule of her ulcerous eyes.
The nervous stutter of her hairlipped mouth. Even the
calcium tusk of her bole did not prevent him returning
for a second look. Three times the cock crowed...!

With a quick survey of the neighbourhood he quickly
ambushed the highly-strung *Elephant girl*. Her
gratitude at being invited back to the neat limits of
his enclosure caused her endless skids of mirth.

She nodded along behind as he charged over the hump of
Buckhurst hill and entered his premises through the
back door...

When he had her safely sitting on the settee he
offered her a glass of milk to soothe her chaffing
throat. As he bent over to offer the glass F. was able
to see for himself the nature of her nauseous
abnormalities.

A thin brown pate of wispy ravel hair covered a
squashed *pygmy* head elongated at the front. Her eyes
were a hazy shade of pink, and her nose was flattened
by a council mallet. Her reading age was certainly
well below average...

Only her hands seemed to have escaped the natural
debacle, her rib cage was twisted and her chest was
'off.' But even those seemed flawed from the outset.
She attempted to blow a kiss but her anomalous teeth
would not co-operate. Certainly onto a 'winner.'

"You do like me don't you?" she entreated. The
factory girls had their fun on the loom.

There was something terribly sad about the 'Elephant
Girl'. Surely, only 'bad witches' were exceedingly
ugly!?' And good ones were, well, most of all pretty!?

Her rancorous cheeks were red and she looked as if
she had been wearing the willow.

He patted *Bog-roll-breath* gently on the shoulder and
put his arm around to show he was not such a monster
too...her breath stank like the dank subway and one
could have planted spuds in her ears.

"What do you want me to do? I don't know what you
want me to do!" she lamented. "My mum wouldn't like it
if I played anything rude." She frowned. "I don't
know if I should..it's been a long time since I married
the little boy next door."

The Flash knelt down before the *Elephant girl* and
rested her disfigurement on his pectorals. If he could
persuade the creature to trust him he might be in a
position to take advantage. For an instant her *baboon*
eyes glittered with a tinsel point of warmth.

"Don't fret my love," he told her. "I'll give you
clear instructions.

Besides, there's no need to tell your mother. It's
funny, but I feel as if I've known you all my life...!"
     "I've been feeling so downhearted," she sobbed.
Tears of joy began to pour down her garish skin and she
hugged her *acrochordus javanicus* fondly over his crown.
     "Never mind. Everything's alright now, eh!" Her
barrel chest convulsed with jocund happiness.
     Her rabid hysteria was gone but still something
troubled the anxious 'Elephant Girl.' Now she was in a
more relaxed frame of mind...
     "Why did you say it wasn't you at the bus stop?" she
quizzed. Her awry chipmunk mouth quivered as she
spoke. There was hardly a joke in it.
     The strange overhanging protuberance of her
consumptive head leaned over the swab deck below him.
"It's quite a show piece isn't it," she gleamed. "What
do you want me to do with it." Need you ask?
     Her sourdough hand reached charyly forward to grip
the nose of his extending trunk. She gradually changed
her tune.
     The distasteful *Elephant girl* promptly bellowed for
air with her eyelids fluttering petulantly.
     "It's far too big to fit in my little Chipmunk
mouth," she complained. She opened up her orifice to
demonstrate this assertion before his erect penis,
whose for-skinned plum was well-peeled.
     With her psychological impediment removed she
suddenly realized it would be 'just possible.' She
moved her jaw ever so slightly closed.
     Once more she charged for the W.C. to pull down her
trousers...
     "This isn't getting us very far!" she observed. "I
do like the show so far but where is this finally
leading?"
     My goodness, look at the time...if she missed her
last bus home there would be a severe rap on the
knuckles! *Prince Charming* coerced her at the point of
a sword to study the firework display at very close
range...

Dazed and confused the glazed eyes of the 'Elephant
Girl' dilated to two diminishing pin-holes.

She withdrew her grasp and hung her head in shame
while he finished paddling his own canoe.

"I don't know what you want me to do!" she bleated.
"I suppose you want to go to sleep now?" she
extrapolated...

F. thought that he heard the succinct rattle of his
downstairs postbox. He ventured gingerly forth to moot
this bolt from the blue.

An arrow-head had been hastily drawn...'Love
Vivienne, X.'

VIII
AQUALUNG

The closer time trickled towards the *trysting* hour the
more Jellyman protested and wanted to go home. He
stared manically through his tinted spectacles and
flicked his 'widow's peak' over the blip of his
skullduggery, gripping the pint of bitter in his other
perspiring pad, trembling at the portal.

"Where are they?" he whined. "Let's take a ticket
to ride," he whimpered.

"I don't think they're coming. Did you h-e-a-r the
shipping forecast. They better not be a blot on the
landscape. Nearly bust a gut to be here prompt."

"I don't know how I ever let you get me into this
mess. You wouldn't catch me having to use a dating
agency in a trillion years," he scorned. "I bet
they're all prostitutes anyway. Don't you have any
other friends you can go with on these trips?" he
rankled. "I think I'd rather slit my own throat."

"My mother doesn't have a spare house door key so I
can't stop over for long. I'm not having any of your
lousy 'cast-offs' he threatened...but it was too late,
they had him trapped *like a frightened rabbit.*

Their brightly coloured *landau* came racing round the
castle corner...he accused F. of contributing to his
downfall. Said he was running him to seed.

"Don't get your knickers in a twist...they only
advertised for 'walking companions.' When I met them
at the Academy of Panoramic Arts they seemed quite
frank and friendly."

Had he been worth getting in touch with again F.
wondered. Jelly-retentive threw his rucksack
contemptuously in the boot of their car. It was
certainly going to be no pic-nic.

Even as they approached the campsite it was raining
cats and dogs. Fuck the electoral role.

The Jellyman seemed about to break into an attack of
apoplexy at the prospect of having one of the girls
sitting on his lap that evening.

His only contribution to the conversation was to
announce that he had nothing in common with them. When
F. patted her arm he was being "far too familiar"...

In the harsh downpour of rain the *two of a kind*
struggled to erect their *basket of hay.*

The savage cascade even threatened to destroy the
hardened armadillo shell of lacquer.

"I don't like yours much!" snapped the Jellyman.
"She looks a right frogging wreck."

"I'm really glad you tracked me down. I tried to
trace you after we flitted but I forgot your number."

Like the *Great Eagle* in the sky which feeds on sparks
of light a region of white lifted high above the grey
nadir fog and scoffed above the mountains.

The surrounding landscape was cottoned in a cloud of
frosted glass as the *dalesmen* struggled with the
decrepit canvas and veteran wooden pegs, squelching in
the lake of mud...

Eventually their miserable hovel stood tottering
beside the bonesetter's land of milk and honey.

The *potato men* huddled inside wishing J. had
remembered to pack the cross beam...

Jellyman recalled his bruntish past when he would
leave the boarding school behind to follow his own
crooked path into the *Darby and Joan* club...

Perched in a *half-lotus* on the air-bed the 'wet-
blanket' retrieved his bicycle book and began to
imbibe. Couldn't go to the bottom of the street
without a mackintosh.

He studied his digital watch. "Don't tell me you
need to have another sleep. What's wrong with you? I
thought you were on the up-grade..."

Charging down the lane to the 'Three Peaks Inn' J.
assumed that F. should attempt to do most of the
fratinizing.

The small party made their way into the freezing tap
room and buttoned-up close as an oyster.

"I fell on Penyghent last year," smiled Katey in an
effort to break the ice.

"I hope Penny was alright!" sparked the *short-
circuited* Flash.

The girl coughed and began to descend. She turned
her best side to hide the *blackdot* in her eye from a
childhood pony accident.

"You're arms look as if they belong to someone
else!" she laughed.

"What a blooming *shambles!*" croaked the Jellyman.
He became consumed with the *Pinball*.

But J. explained how the 'Socialist Republic of
South Yorkshire' had recently extended him a contract
to pioneer new cycling routes along 'Old disused
Railway lines' for the next seven years.

He also had to capture the declining viaducts on his
photo-lens while sketching a map of the cloudscape.

Before he developed into de-constructivism and his
'Cat-O-nine-tales.'

'Why did eunuchs never lose their hair?' F. could
only colour. The *million ton heart*.

The whole evening was spent down in the doldrums.
It became clear from that moment on that the Jellyman
was nothing but a damp squib...

F. departed like a skeleton from the feast into the
hail of frogs for it was impossible to blow-out in the
Flashflood.

He opened the swing door for the ladies and cast a
sheep's eye on their intrinsical *rapprochement*.

Jelly suddenly decided to sail ahead into the
caliginous Niagara.

Marching twenty paces ahead of the little group the
Blackdog gradually quickened his pace and soon
disappeared completely out of sight. Perhaps he was on
a mercy mission?

"Your 'best' friend doesn't seem to like us very
much," said Katherine sadly. "Is he always such a
cad?"

"He's depressed because of all this damned rain,"
excreted F., reserving his day of reckoning.
   "Hey fella!" shouted *Flashman* from the darkness.
"You got a problem?" He nearly came a cropper on the
trail of slime.
   They could just discern the snarl of the Jellyman
echoing across the void as he entered the sludge at the
gateway.
   "People asking me if I have a problem!" he snapped
verbosely in his belligerent arrogant manner.

With the dry sheets wrapped underneath his arm F.
charged helter-skelter for the keys to her ripuarian
terrace...by six o-clock, and with the heater pumping
hot, he had been able to have a jolly good foss without
the awful presence of the disturbed Jellyman. The
windows were practically weeping by the time he had
finished spurting.
   He pulled back the flap of his companions' shower
proof scout tent and burst into hysterics. Lying in
the centre of the stage was a sight which made the
complete dive worthwhile.
   Hemming the motionless Jellyman on the life raft
floated a myriad of scrofulitic debris...
   The *Mormon* perlustrated remissly from his island and
splashed his sluicing eyes. His only pelt was a
patchwork quilt of socks. Between the gaps his white-
fish body appeared totally salient.
   "Is it opening time yet?" he instinctively asked.
He feebly insisted his bio-rhythms were on the blink.
   Fitted with all 'mod cons' the girls prepared their
English breakfast behind the convenient protection of
their wind shield. After a comfortable nights rest in
their submarine palace they emerged teed up to wade
through the reign of St. Swithins.
   Before the *pissflap* of their ragged slaver the
smelly fisherman and the churlish *cabinboy* drew straws
to cook their pastiche of conduit junket; mushrooms,
kippers, eggs and tomatoes were all piled high in their
only frying pan, as they shivered cyclonically without
want or reason...

"I'm definitely not pitching my tent again," he vowed. Just as the baked beans were being added to the *belly timber* the single calor gas stove decided to spring its entire board over the bubbling marsh.

He loaded the gunge back into the cooking pot with his bare hand as the deviant flame flickered even in the slightest breeze. After an hour the meal was still only luke warm, then the bottle decided to give up the ghost with one last...'Pop!' What a stroke of luck they were having. Bring on the last straw!

The girls had gathered booted and spurred, equipped to march into oblivion.

F. shook his head. "We'll skip it today I think," he said. "The *Jellyman* feels unwell after his recent *mastication*. If we detect any change in the climate, we'll catch you up at *Three Mile Cross*...Okay!"

Jelly watched them turn and wave in the *waterspout* as they rounded the five bar with a gushing sense of relief. He was still addicted to the weed...that much was obvious, and waded in 'duck's wine.'

Deep red blotches appeared on his neck and arms even before F. asked him why he had been such a pillock.

After the flood he fertilized the earth with his thoughts. His gramaphone needle slid across the disc. A 'mallingerer' fretted that he had been dragged there under false pretences.

"I'm as 'Mad as a Hattersley!'" he fumed. "You should never ever have brought me to this watershed!" he screamed. Jelly seemed to be overwhelmed by impossible odds. Like three daffs in a jam jar.

"Did you see her," he groaned, grabbing F.'s arm and rolling like a pig in the pen.

"Did you see that girl? She had a grey hair on her head, and she was only twenty-nine. I saw it there!"

He pandered ferociously and kicked over the tent pole...

"I'm absolutely pogged!" he hissed.
The 'needs of the one, far out-weighed the needs of the many.'

                    *   *   *

Before a sparkle of light the black sky opened wide
from the leaky tin pail and F. knew that it was time to
ply the oars once more.

In only a T-shirt and jeans our hero mounted his
trusty rusty bike and darted over the blip of the hill
in the dense December torrent.

Huge drops of *aqua vitae* bounced on his bare bonce
as his denim distended like a heavy sponge.

After throwing his bike outside the check-out it was
no surprise to find a youth sprinting into the distance
when he returned.

F. gave chase towards the long lane of condemned
buildings.

When he rounded a corner he was able to observe his
front wheel being buckled and the spokes snapped...it
was too much hassle to prosecute. Shouts of 'Egghead!'
from the bus-stop...

Just as the mariner was shielding his eyes from the
dam he even managed to crash headlong into a parked car
again, and tumbled over the bonnet from the windscreen.

The motorist watched in amazement as the street
artist rapidly bent his bicycle frame back into shape
and straightened up the forks, intent on riding into
the horizon, bobbing up and down on the wonky sprag.

As he travelled under the arch beside the 'Cap and
Bells' a shower of missiles plummeted from above.

A flintstone was embedded in his forehead at the
point where the dancing girl had been screwed in her
Grandfather's summer clunker during bacchanalia.

Following the line of quaint slate cottages where
the row of decaying barges stood F. trundled
determinedly over the ridges of the rodway where the
anglers fished on blind men's holidays.

A huge puddle spread completely across the track,
but he flew right through sending a spray of mud
shooting over his back.

The distant hum of the chemical works still clogged the discordant sky with a torch of tyrant flame. He'd been chased the previous night for pedalling blindfold.

The pedlar persevered towards the buckler where the fauna unfolded like a sodden *garden of Eden*.

Shaking his dice in a pint-gallon cup he flung them against the violent sea of spray.

His darkroom timer began to fright as he ploughed along the old straight track with the wind beating fiercely agin im. Whims of the not so young.

The yellow lantern glimmered weakly through the *Cider* Wood as he fought bravely against the baser elements, drawing him like a magnet towards the cove of Stamford.

He navigated the *oar-scull* where the mute swans had taken refuge in the banking, and a Barn Owl suddenly appearing in the branch above him had made his heart beat much faster then.

The stellar motion gleamed like mica overhead as chalkdust nodded to its fall through the glass bottle recently shaken...

Our wayfarer approached the spinney gate with his head swimming, below the rising moon coruscating on the silver ripples of the horse-shoe bend.

The raven shadow of a silent punt bubbled like a barm of thistle down through the clutching mist with its ghostly troupe of randan fugitives.

A small trail of mustard gas crooned from the summit of Neptune's chimney as he picked his way through the bare blackberry bushes teeming in the ether.

Just as he was equating the hedgerow to hog the wooden rampart F.'s bicycle chain snapped with a 'twang' of *feu de joie*...the cyclist jogged the last few yards over the gravel bed with the contraption under his arm.

He hesitated by the coal bunker to rip-off the plastic bin-liners ensconced with rubber bands, and clanked over the cinders to call on his relief still bantering on the telephone at the top, and filled with profligate vitriol.

"Jesus Fucking Christ!" he cursed as he entered the Slime-house door and flung his only viable transport angrily against the barrier.

With 'blood and water' pouring into his eyes the deviant *Flash* hobbled over to the condensated pendant where his large red moustache had accumulated a frosty coat of salt...

Old Nick Sunderland turned as if he'd just fallen out of the wrong side.

"*Inspector Clouseux* has been spying on his friends again from the bushes on the village 'green.' He wants you to lend him your bicycle pump for his blow-up doll," he sneered.

"He's old as 'Methusaleh,'" the stool pigeon sniggered and sloshed his tipple of brandy from an egg cup.

The droll jade eyes suddenly sprang into second gear as he interrogated the Flasher on his whereabouts and his wanking pit.

"Why do you always have to be such a bleeding weatherboard!" he wittered in his monotone.

"Whaaaa... time do you call this?" he moaned. "I wouldn't pay you in frigging cardboard washers."

The *fossilized icyathorus* swung his spastic legs over the checked woollen blanket and placed his shawl obediently in the carrier bag...

'When-the-boat-comes-in' cranked his stiff metal neck anti-clockwise, and peered weakly through his vacant hamster eyes towards the Flash dripping from head to foot.

The copious stare intensified as he complained about the *Salamander* being nothing but a dingy dustbowl when he had relieved him earlier that sunrise.

Shuffling drearily in the dismal light of the covenant with his distempered hand recoiling against his sworn enemy the auxiliary pilotman removed his unholy slippers and placed them carefully in his leather service bag behind the safe-keeping of the locker.

His famous quickslime was wrapped up tight in the
remains of a senior glass-cloth and disposed of beneath
the eave of the Signalling frame when F. turned his
back for a moment.

As he pulled on his fabrikoid ulster he complained
bitterly about the discrepencies of the dosser and his
constant prey on the mind.

He perambulated vicariously towards the entrance
dragging his weak left side behind him and a race-track
of short expletives.

"We've had a complete power failure, but I don't
suppose you're really that bothered," he conceded
impishly. "'Time Interval Working' in operation," he
susurrated. "I've 'ad to use t' oil lamps and t' coyls
in't bucket. If you want some more watter you'll 'ave
to give em a bell up at' Bridge to send additional
containers on the next down train."

The old man's tooth had faded eerily in his helmet
as he wambled in the doorway and tripled his sarcastic
barrage.

"Well, just look at you!" he mattocked joyfully, as
if his mouth were full of humbugs. His lurid
expression shone in the moonlight. "Did ya fall in the
canal?" he bloomed.

Mounting the thick leather gloves on his over-
exposed fingers Old Nick stared wryly down at the pool
of water gathering on the floor and reminded the
Flasher to mop it up before he returned in the heimal.

"What ya need is a damned good waterproof to go with
all this rain," he gleamed. Salt water welled in his
eyes.

Then he winked instructively and nodded down the
line.

"I bet if ya flashed that there home signal 'all on'
against the 'Flying Scotsman' crossing the points, and
threw the Crossover in reverse...ten to one 'e would
de-rail im!"

"But don't try it, will you lad?" he stressed, heavy
with melancholia...

The old copper kettle giggled merrily on the ferrous
hob as the Signalman removed all his clothes and spread
them neatly round the cast-iron fireplace.

Even the plastic bags around his ankles had to be
turned inside out where the perspiration had recently
fermented.

Through the tiny rear window he peered out across
the waterlogged farmer's field toward the prehistoric
carmine forest incapsulating the cemetery, and the
dower-house beyond the nepenthe river winding its way
toward humane civilization.

Every kind of creature called and stirred in the
wilderness. A fruit bat was seen gliding among the
perennial shrub and a kestrel twirling in the bowery of
mare's tail hovered before alighting on the primeval
fences. Three long winters trekking to the *nature
reserve* had brought but a pigmy prestige, and the only
regular gain was *gut rot*.

He could hear the braying of the garrulous donkey
crepitating over the moat as the herd of cattle
congregated near the ploughshare...then they were all
struck dumb.

The telephone rang; it was Peter Farley to give him
a detailed description of the portions which he'd
scrunched at the Red Lion during lunchtime.

"A word of warning!" he purred. "*Nana Sahib* is on
the prowl so keep on calling *attention*. You know how
he's out to make a name for himself."

"Oh take no notice of that snide old bugger!" he
laughed, and burst into a rendition of his favourite
passage.

"'Please to remember the fifth of November, for
gunpowder, treason and plot. I see no reason why
gunpowder treason should ever be forgot!'"

"Don't you ever become another Alexander Selkirk,"
exhorted the lonely mesial bachelor. A former 'Punch
and Judy' extrovert.

"I left it all too late, silly sod. Now listen
carefully and take my advice," he harkened cautiously;

"It all depends what value you put on yourself. Find a
nice little wife and settle down, then I can pop over
for tea and crackers!" he chuckled.

The good Inspector with a voice like box of noisy
tin tacks blasted excitedly down the megaphone.

"Though I'm not past it yet! I can still do the
things you young fella's can," he postulated (Old Nick
always made wise cracks about him being a fifety-two
year old virgin.)

"Peter, you're like a father to me," declared the
deplorable Flasher.

"Give me a release for the branch...did I tell you
I'm supposed to be playing football a week on Saturday
for *Psycho* and his mob...but I'll have to give my poor
neighbour a ring soon. That's the third time this week
I've left my keys in the front door!"

"I'm thinking of building an Ark if this keeps up!
How many weeks has it been now?"

His tone sounded altogether softer. The highly
strung *Bobby* had always dined with *Duke Humphrey* ever
since the tar and feathering while on national
service...anxiety about his small proportions had added
to his gross exaggeration.

Nick was heard to promulgate that he reckoned it
wouldn't be long until he was admitted permanently to
the 'funny farm.' That they were reserving a place
especially for him in the padded cell...it seemed.

"It's like a Dannemora!" blasted the boisterous
foghorn. "We've been sentenced to break rock. What
other jobs do you know where you have to sit on your
fat arse all day long without a decent remission."
Then he complained about his *diverticular*. He had been
down the steps three times already and he hadn't been
able to pass stools.

"I've burnt all that filthy smut," he tumulted. "If
they turn up with any more the same thing will happen
to them too!"

"I need your urgent advice," he raged deliriously.
"When I shuffle off this mortal coil, do you think I
should be buried, or *cremated?* They say that fire is
far more edulcorate."

"When I think how dear mother joined the invisible choir," he fretted. "All I desire is to die with my boots on..."

After removing his spectacle lens the celibate began blubbering into his sweat-rag and blowing his bill.

Peter Farley described how he had joined-up with his *swain departed* in a recent bugbear. Hopping the twig on the branch line they had suddenly dived down a hole in the *hiatus maxime*.

"They're in and out of that cess-pit like a bloody don't know what," he recoiled. "It'll be reyt!"

"I'll tap you in time to play the 'dawn chorus' as usual," he sighed, and slammed down the hearing aid like a gun-shot.

The leeching sleet soon cavalried to fiercesome blizzard summoning 'Big George' Bush the *Snowman* on his tiny scooter to the country Glasshouse.

With the Junction points freed of ice trains could run smoothly over the branch, or be operated manually by the cranking handle at the groundframe.

Waggling the penis in his hand as the rush-hour commuter bullited below the window *Big George the Snowman* removed every last stitch and paraded round the room weighing his scrotum.

"Now you know why they call him 'Big George!'" chattered 'Chalky White' in awe, and agreed it was a mighty weapon too...

The blower rattled the catch. It was the 'phantom trumpeter' again. He blew a raspberry in the Flasher's ear and hurriedly volleyed the call.

"It's for you George...I think that it's your supervisor to find out if you've finished quaffing at the Salty Dog yet."

Holding the receiver in his hand his flesh steamed beside the red hot trivet.

"Hello boss," he said, as Chalky ran for cover. "Hey Gilbert, where on earth are you...?"

"There's method in their madness!" he said...

A snowball fight left the refuge covered in a vista of wet projectiles...

Before the Sanding engine arrived to spread its gum over the surface of the gradient F. disposed of the sour apples which had been slaking on the iron-bound shingle.

Mixing the chunks with a bag of granulated sugar he unlocked the latch of the chamber and abandoned the frosty giants thawing by the pot.

In the hush of night the *Neanderthal man* was giving his clandestine impressions of a Pterodactyl.

Those chronic escapades tapping the bolts with his P.Way hammer had eventually landed him at the twenty mile post. They all pretended he had them fooled again...

F. clomped down to the basement with the pan in his grasp. Here the charcoaled remains of Sylvester's old bird-table still projected from the dreary archipelago.

Consumed with canine madness Martin had danced around the totem with the paraffin can while it simooned.

The *deep-sea plunger* crunched over the dessicate mound of polar grains as Haley's comet heralded from behind the torpid image.

Sodium chloride had been scattered on the *bifrost* bridge where the Signalman called out loud for the created being across the freezing arctic.

He caught the distant whinnying as he braced, and began to dash across the open space with his hooves athunder...

Elydour broke into a slow trot as he approached the wooden stile, with his long plumed tail bristling like a line of white hot filaments.

The sore red eyes contrasted sharply with the blissful crescent shape.

He plodded gently over the last few paces to receive his sweet with breath expiring like a *Bengal* vapour.

"See you tomorrow son," he vowed. But the liver-chestnut had gone to meet his maker...

Big George had graced himself with a pair of slippers when he arrived back in the hot-house. He became increasingly aggressive when F. refused to arm wrestle him.

"With your physique you ought to be on the screen," he tempered. "What is the girth of your buttocks? We heard about you carrying a full cylinder across the road on your tod...pound for pound you must be one of the strongest men in England."

As the lion lay down with the lamb for peace in still water the Flash caved in to their request. He shoulder pressed a *scrap of Ironhorse* sixty times above his head to prove his point. 'Not until I'm absolutely perfect,' he deemed.

"How is it that you can't even net a slag?" asked George curiously. The only lifting Big George did was with his right hand.

"The company have all heard the stories about the *mad Lampman roaming the Eastern Region with his can open.*"

F. blushed and stuttered his way over to the boiler...er!

"Okay if I leave some of our dets in the cupboard for emergencies?" asked the Snowman.

"That's alright by me," sniffed the Flash. "As long as they do not come into contact with moisture or 'Chloride of Lime,' and are kept in a clean plastic container."

When he opened the door for them to depart for *Buckland tunnel* to clear the icicles hanging from its roof Billy Goat Gruff was chewing an old boot in the middle of the track.

A *pair of Snowmen* chased the tribe of seven back inside the entrance having forgotten to Scotch the points.

Peter Farley rang to air his feelings. With his pet poodle cradled fondly on his lap he protested at the ban from visiting his young niece.

"I've had another call from that disgusting pervert the 'Phantom Trumpeter.' Something should be done about his flagrant molestation."

Nancy had just had another operation costing several hundred smackers. Her paws never touched the ground even in the mildest of weather-ships.

Suddenly the Signalling Inspector's van screeched to a
halt outside the glass cabin.

F. quickly finished washing his slippery penis in
the drinking bottles. He dried himself on Nick's old
dish-rag.

The amateur Rugby player bounded up the stairs and
burst in through the door with sirens blaring, at four
o-clock in the trance of winter gloom.

The baby-faced *inquisitor* dressed in black
immediately directed his cohorts to search the box for
'training' weights...occasionally forestalled by the
ticing of his eye-lid.

"*Out-of-hours visit*," grinned the youthful 'Poacher
turned Gamekeeper.' "Are you by any chance in
possession of an illegal radio set?"

"What do you think of your new mate?" he asked the
resident Signalman; referring to the son of one of the
local nags.

"You mean do I approve of *nepotism* on the railway?"
asked the Flashman.

Bowie appeared unprepared for this assertive
comment. The newlywed's lanner-glance swept the
perimeter of the establishment for signs of further
shotten herring.

In places the planks were splintered.
"Management potential," he leered. "Should go far
also!"

"You're a square peg in a round hole," hissed the
intermediary.

He complacently stiled his name over the entries and
noted down the time exactly in his diary. Apparently
you were 'never to mention' the reasons for his
promotion.

"Have you ever thought of an occupation *Off the
Railway?*" he hootingly remarked. "How are your hands
with a shovel?"

"That is not for you to comment on, and is a clear
case of supererrogation," replied the Flasher.

"Why haven't you put the amendments in your 'Rule
Book!'" he scoffed.

"I warned you only yesterday! *Do it now!*" he demanded
menacingly.

Bowie walked over to the cooker and threw out the
grilling tray...he made his point felt.

"Uugh! That is disgusting!" he cried. "Don't you
ever buck the bloody twat? J. Arthur Rank! Is it you?
Why is there such a godawful stale odour?"

"I checked the *Bardic Lamp* only the other evening,"
he sneered. "Could you tell me in your own words why
there was no battery therein. Your mate said that you
nicked it to attach to the front of your bone-shaker.
Is that correct? What would have happened if he needed
to use it in an avalanche? Don't you dare sell me down
the river."

"Of course not!" shivered the Flash. "If I know
Slag Heaps he was probably using it for his wrangler
when you whistled to a dead stop."

"That is pure guesswork!" stuttered Bowie smartly.
"You'll be hearing from the Regional Supremo about this
very shortly I can promise you."

When the blower suddenly barked Bowie grabbed the
receiver.

With a wry smile the muddy *Man in Black* turned to
take his charge into custody.

Browsing through the log for a moment F. stared
quickly back to instill his true expression...with his
left eye twitching fiendishly the Inspector strode
manfully across the frieze with his black *jackboots*
squeaking salaciously.

The odious *gestapo* convened back to the yellow van
to await further instructions, while their chief knelt
down to pry inside the private parts.

He burst from the shelf like a firecrack.
"What are these fucking dets doing in here? Get the
fuck out!" he addered. Bowie went straight off the
deep end. Language which was totally UNPRINTABLE!

Meanwhile the Signalman in charge had filled in the
time for 'Train-Out-of-Section' for the passing Sanding
Engine in one column.

Bowie dusted his military type uniform and marched
dutifully across the rogue floor capsizing on the patch
of lotion which had been spilled near the water pails.

"Aha! Just like your 'mate' predicted!" he chanted,
with a self-satisfied smug lighting up his snapper.

"Pre-booking by two minutes...you're *nabbed!*"
He accurately circled the entry and prepared to
withdraw the register for closer examination on his
swivel chair at the laboratory.

Bowie chuckled to himself as he waltzed plyently to
the exit. He made as if to walk down the steps, and
pointed towards the banking which lurched down to the
congealed bight of alph-alpha floating beneath the hazy
screen of gauze.

"I can *walk on fucking water, I can!*" he bragged.
"What the hell's all those bloody milk cartons doing
down there and where did that pile of baked bean cans
come from? Can't you incinerate them or something.
You'll be attracting filthy vermin!" he snarled dryly.

"I've seen plenty of sewer-sloppers around here
already," admitted the Flash. "I happen to work with a
few earwiggers..."

At the *adjacent box* Bowie rushed feverishly to
report his findings to the *Generalissimo* asleep at home
in bed.

The enthusiast could hardly contain his delight as
the black-gloved-hand trembled on the end of his knob.

"Two whole minutes!" he said. "We've really got him
this time!"

"*A booking error...*" sniffed the other one coldly.
"That's a most serious offence. In the case of a
Signalman we'll certainly have to open all the sluices.
So *Old Nick* was right then? Well done Mr. Bowie!
We'll have him on the carpet before the ink is dry.
I'll have the form one typed out at once..." The In-
law turned to his secretary.

The Inspector replaced the hearing device and spun
round in a flurry of ebullition bolstering his
forefinger in a halo above his noddle.

"*A Dangerous Man!*" blared Peter Farley excitedly in
his blatant foghorn thud.

He picked his lug with the but of a matchstick stalk
and then he scratched his crease.

"And they call some men animals," he shrieked. "Well,
I think that's a flipping insult to living beasts."

"If your face fits," he wheezed. "Aaaha...flipping
ummer! He's always getting his knife into
someone...that's *work harassment!*" he yelped.

"Give a dog a bad name. Why can't they just pull
our pants down and give us six of the best over the
sink. Then it's all over and done with. I'll be glad
to sign your petition. It's been a real pleasure
working with you lad when you've been breasting the
current. Even Harold Bentiron received a pardon in
nineteen fifty-seven when the guard was killed by a
steamer rolling forward at *Caution.*"

"There was only one man deemed to be *perfect,*" he
said, "and look what they did to him."

Then F. confided about the melted Bardic...
"Nay lad, I've been forty year without them throwing
out confetti" he choked. "You can get to the bottom of
a thief, but you can *never* get to the bottom of a liar!
I can't wait to get away from here today," he soaked.
"It's driving me up the wall. I hope you're not
crashing down in the Signalbox all weekend again.
You're better off at home...and remember, go straight
there," he prayed. "Don't stop anywhere along the
way...even to have a P."

As it neared sundown in the ring of bright water the
batchelor's archaic moped rattled along the ridge of
the canal bank opposite on its way to the wall above
Blubberhouses.

Silhouetted against the scarlet sunset his figure
clumsily negotiated the obstacles of splintered rock
and peered every so often across the valley to his
younger protege.

The biker's hoary wig drifted from his battle helmet
in the gale as he bruised against the chips of vitreous
with his corpulent body perched comically above the
thin metallic wafer...

F. threw himself to the floor and tried to disguise
his stroke of policy...

For three whole days during stoppage time he lay low
and continued to survive in his second cantonment.

The only mortals he saw were the rambling geriatrics
marching in single file along the bizarre pontoon.
They all greeted him in turn as if they had seen him
there for years, then they too evaporated down the
line.   There wasn't even a whiff of that 'Secret
Commomwealth.'

Singing, screaming, kicking, raving - "Whose making
that din?" someone asked.   Then he remembered to
replace the phone on the hook.   "There's no reason why
anyone should be alone in this day and age..."

But before another phase had passed he was breaking
into block again with the required 7.5.5 bell signal.

He adjusted the lever to slack and rang the S + T
Technician via Control, who arranged for the 'Emergency
Call Out' team.

As agreed the technician flashed his headlights on
rounding the far corner.

In the distance *Galen* scrambled to the top of the
gantry and carefully examined the equipment like a tiny
sparrow on the washing pole.

On arriving in the moored tourniquet he logged his
time in the register; it was double time for
Sundays..."Nothing found!" he winked.

"Go on, take the money love," he pricked.   "I said
I'd make it worth your while.   I'll buy you a bottle of
advocar at your convenience!"

Galen was soon shooting back to his resting-place.
It would be nightfall until the Flash saw another
living soul so he decided to *dub* all four phones with
shoe polish out of sheer boredom, rather than revenge.

A cold pail of water was co-ordinated to the front
door with a trip wire while he glanced through his copy
of *Twenty thousand leagues under the Sea*.

It was after midnight just before the Signalbox was
due to shut that F. suddenly noticed sharp shadows
parading rudely over the bastille walls as a speeding
crate bounced along the rocky private tract.

His heart dropped as the pale faced *growler* paced
out of the dog-cart and came marching circumspectly up
the stairs.

The Station Manager stood waiting nervously outside the
door until he had closed the joint 'locked by the
block.'

"If you really want to know, I think they've handled
this all wrong," he mused, as the frescoed Signalman
fastened up the shelter. He tentatively stepped
outside the protection of his dun and placed the key
underneath the rug.

Gilbert's double efficiently delivered him the 'Form
1' with the charge neatly printed on the front page now
that he was definitely 'off duty.' It was simply a
matter of procedure.

F. humbly accepted the apocryphal parchment.
"I'm sorry mate," sighed Gilbert. "You're last form
one. I don't know why but they certainly have it in
for you. I'll give you a lift back most of the way if
you like."

"No thankyou," knelled the Flasher.
He soberly viewed the manager take in sail along the
track of golden mean with the two beams of light rising
and falling with the milky landscape.

Even though it meant jogging half starved the twelve
miles home to emptyness with his bicycle slung over his
shoulder it could give him an opportunity to masturbate
outside those alluring cottage portals.

Who knew what he might see. If there was a balm of
blue sky his wife would forget to pull on her
curtains...couples fucking on the bank. Nearly came a
cropper.

Setting the fire for the night he tidied up the
Signalbox and disconnected his *Bugging Device* from the
circuit telephone.

Mounting the ladder through an alchemy of nature the
chill-blamed kid flew amid the murky feral woods as if
the power of air was giving him the bends.

Between singing extracts of 'Vincent' he communed
speeches of his own as he navigated the *Maelstrom brim*
crammed with mildewed moth and rust:

> Ten winds climb the top of me
> Damn I the threatening score
> Of traffic zooms the ears with wrath
> As I tread the vly in stones...

He could have sworn the Section Signal was still
displaying danger but there was no chance of turning
tide. What problem could there have been if *Psycho* had
given him the release correctly? Although there was a
suspicion he had long needed a pair of decent
spectacles... and paused at the chevron of the distant
Semaphore during fair to middling snow.

Suddenly a dark figure appeared moving silently
toward him in the midst of those frightening woods. At
that time of night? He shuddered and attempted to keep
his distance.

Was the stranger riding a bicycle. He seemed to
glide quickly over the physical features. F. began to
speed-up as the figure past him, taking a singular
glance at this unusual starling. Then he ran like the
clappers. Broken chains!

Dressed in a long dark cloak the *Boatman* was wearing
a 'First World War' Gas mask and invisible below his
knees...raced for his 'four-poster.'

Dripping wet with condensation after more than two
hours on the open road the Flasher approached the
International Sports Stadium knowing he was nearing
home, territory.

He decided to free wheel down the hill, only to be
passed by a 'Petrol tank Wanker' waving his finger.

The motorist rounded the bollards and sculled
purposefully back to flatten him into the kerb...he
skated up the mound prepared to take his shower.

When he gushed inside the suburban *Shoebox* the
telephone was still ringing.

He rushed to pick up the receiver slinging his
useless caravan under the downstairs spiral.

Was there a last minute hitch, or had they abruptly
decided to run a special unit through the leaking
passage of pipe?

Had *Harry Morgan blobbed* and they wanted him to cover?
He half expected to hear the Inspector's turbulent
voice railing at him from the 'Flossie.' There was
hesitation on the part of the incumbent. Eyup!
'Phantom Trumpeter,' he thought.

"What?" commented F. as the Station Supervisor at
the *Terminus* recited his name and number. "You're
joking. When did this take place?"

"A letter? There at the station...what state is he
in? But that was years ago..."

Dick Baldbeard chuckled cruelly among his cronies.
He insisted that the *sleeveless errand* would certainly
not be allowed to strike root on the platform slabs
until sunrise.

Could he shoot-down immediately to collect the web-
footed Red Star contusion before it became marasmus.

Catch a falling star, put it in your pocket, save it
for a rainy day...

!   !   !

Mary angrily blew her top and accused him of having
muddied the *waters'* of *pacification.*

"If you have anything to do with him you can say
goodbye to all that's in my certificate of probate. He
will only drag you down to his low level." But just
how low could he eventually sink?

In the hazy spin of the quarter moon F. watched from
the window as the taxi arrived.

The cabbie helped the *invalid out* with 'No fixed
abode.'

Like a man of constant sorrow the traveller seemed
unsure which direction he was taking to reach rock
bottom.

He floundered anxiously as they fumbled the steely
vine of ice into the holt below the windowpane.

Walking men in buckram and desolate he emerged from
the mists of Pre-history like a faded *daguerrotype.*

Attempting to makaton a white flag he staggered
dazed and confused from the peat bog gesturing mutely
on a silent promenade.

The *anachronism* addressed his pockets for an up-to-
date space map but seemed totally overawed by the
occassion. Vatter' on't brain. Earlugs water-logged.

From where F. stood it was impossible to see if he
had begun weeping.

His scarlet hooter had been split in half by a
workman's pick-axe, and his leg wound still made
walking extremely harrowing.

Creepy Kevin perched on the communal bannister-rail
sight-seeing.

After regarding the man rocking up the steps he
peered through a small gap in his door and then closed
it just as quickly as the squad approached.

Still rattling the sabre above his head the Shadow
remarked how much he had altered during the marching of
the clock.

F. cooked him his first decent meal in weeks and sat
him in the wicker chair.

The last vestige of the primordial ocean swung and
extended his arms as if denouncing a Jezebel. But F.
couldn't seem to fathom out what he was talking about.
He'd never shaved another man before, but he would have
to start somewhere...his vertigo had been diagnosed by
Doctor Parkinson as incurable. He fed him with a spoon
much in his own likeness.

'Why did he decide to cross the channel all those
years ago?' he asked.

The *Shadow* grinned. "W-w-well, the fare to the
beach was only a tanner cheaper an' I thought, why not,
there's nothing to lose," he stammered. Would Mary
fill in his UB40 for him?

At the bottom of his suitcase was a charcoal drawing
and an appointment card. It was long overdue. Then he
murmurred something about *the-lid-of-Mide*.

The man groped for the gifts of foreign paper strewn
around the floor...but F. refused at first.

Even though his business overdraft was sinking him
slowly he suggested the man buy himself a reasonable
sou'wester. His punts were for all those O-levels.
And A-levels? Were they a kick upstairs?

Apparently he also carried something in his chest
for Mary and her Bodger but he wouldn't be specific,
although he seemed confident they would be impressed by
its sharpness.

When he lifted his turn-up the scar still ran like a
rake sword with its open edge of red.

It wept a continuous stream of venom under his
saturated cloth. A stink of sulphur stang along his
pride and his outer scratch was laced with purple. 'If
I had a batchelor pad like this,' he grimaced.

Then he excused himself to administer his tube of
haemorrhoid ointment. The *Shadow* pulled a ghastly face
as he returned...but his breath still smelled of
spirits.

"P-p-pissing blood again today," he asserted.
"Still a good dick though!" he smiled.

"Up the Provisionals," he cheered.

"Up the bloody I.R.A.!" Swore they'd planted something
big in Trafalgar Square...The apostle of the whiskey
bottle had a fiery glow about his ruddy cheeks and his
eyes were certainly starry.

Like a set of dominoes propelled by 'cause and
effect' the *woodman* was imprisoned in the barrel of his
sinking ship. Thrown by every wave....

"Gi us a job," he begged; his blue eyes blinking
mercifully. Do you think you could put in a good word?
"G-g-g-gis a job," he stammered painfully.

"I'm never going to see you again," he wailed.
The Shadow growled, F. flinched, and cowered back
instinctively.

"I don't suppose your mother would ever have a thick
Irish navvy like me!" he admitted resignedly.

He desperately wanted to be assured that all was
well and that the lynch law were not arriving to
sanction his *ducking underwater.*

The *Shadow* began to sob out loud and jerked his head
just like some of the patients he used to tease.

With an expression of sheer terror he trembled with
trepidation as the train gathered speed receding into
the tunnel-mouth.

Holding the tickets in his tenuous grip his
shrinking eyes flowed in and out of the seating.

All around him the passengers viewed with a passive
indifference his descent into the *waters of oblivion.*

The telephone rang at after midnight. F. could
hardly believe his ears...

"No money left in his pockets? *Ferry across the
Mersey!*"

The Sergeant described how they had found him
wandering drunkenly along the docks without a penny to
his name. He'd long since missed the crossing and the
boat coupons had been flogged.

"I'm flabbergasted," snapped the Flash. "What's to
be done now?"

"Don't worry," whispered the caller. "We'll see
that your father gets home alright even though he
doesn't seem to know the time of day."

'He's the best father I ever had,' said F.

A fool and his money were quickly parted.

"When you dine with the devil you sup with a very long
spoon."

Still a few tricks up his sleeve?

Who the hell cared about Danny. Not even Danny cared
about Danny anymore...dead, dead, and never call him
father.

IX

SAID THE WIND TO BEVIS

He bade farewell to the language students from Berlin
and departed the empty tube at King's Cross laden for
the Youth Hostel at Holland Park. The German frauline
had been extremely interested in the manoeverings of
his zipper...but they left each other anyway and
continued on their separate causeways.

"Yah! The *Mad Pandemic Surgeon.* Everyone at the
wall has heard of the redlights of ST. PETER'S BURG."

Had not the self-styled genius failed his 11-plus he
would undoubtedly have been an old boy. So close yet
so far the Flasher paraded from the exit...

After last orders in the bright lights of the West
End bar he had suddenly found the nanny was a *Titan*
when she stood up from the table.

He was deserted all alone on the pavement spinning
round in circles until the arrival of the rescue party
travelling home from the festival.

The Jellyman had bolted from the snug assuming their
verbal intercourse was an absolute waste of time. What
narked him the most was his comatose appreciation of
the brass tacks. His moods were growing daily. It
certainly wasn't their friendship.

Having completely lost his sense of direction F.
hollered down a passing Panda car.

"You can take a short cut through the alley," winked
the hooded *man in black.* "But don't linger under a
blue moon near the palings!"

He crossed the road with a single thought preying on
his mind. How soon before he could relieve himself?
Perhaps there was a streak of phosphor shining from the
ladies' dormitories? Would he be able to consumate his
act without the springs of his bunk-bed clattering?

136

Had he or had he not heard another restless sigh in the darkness as he passaged to the bog-maker's hut? Could he fish up a new clue by hunting round the kedge with his rod and tackle?

The igloo was sending a tingle down his spine. Hadn't the warden the right of veto? His guests appeared an extremely odd variety.

Spaced every few yards along the raven curling pathway malingered the band who studied his approach with arrogant derision.

He flew like an arrow through the air of burden. Were the *smoking Jesuits* intending to give him aggro?

In the deathlike pallour of the clam sirocco breeze F. hesitated as the *figure* smiled beneath a spotlight in the distance.

He decided to take a good look at her as he passed to see if he could ascertain in which queer club she was an operative.

A strong sexual climate maundered in the high pressure zone as the fellow loitered whispering with the leaves.

The blonde pouted as he beadled by and shuffled back to his impure patch of fosse on being thrown overboard.

As F. shuddered with alarm he quickly rounded the corner by the *swastika* and made the welkin ring over the cobbles. Was some ancient sacrifice being made? Who were the gay young men hustling in the cockshut? At last he reached blighty just as Helga was emerging from the dry room.

"I wouldn't go down that lane if I were you!" warned the Flash. "There really are some weird characters on the loose."

When he entered the annex the *Spineless one* seemed already asleep in his sleeping bag on the ramshackle trencher.

The Garden Gnome was still snarling in his bowl. All his worldly goods were stored in the old tin pram at the pier end of his bed-post and the pole-cat stench was practically a provocation to do his head in.

When F. turfed over his mattress the Jellyman babbled
about a rise in the tide. He wriggled and gnashed his
teeth.

"You'll be like that one day," he gratefully
foretold. "Although I always wanted to be a tramp
myself when I grew up. What did you want to be?   A
shower curtain in a girls' boarding school?"

"Put a sock in it!" snapped the Flash, as the warden
noctivagated by the gap flickering his torch.

He counted the number of drips from the tap before
cruising into the pool hall.

"I told you we should have paid!" wailed the
Jellyman dispersing his upheaval among the *sack of
toads.*

*   *

The Flashman posted a dozen copies of the 'great' 'new'
'Spot the Virgin' competition to his employers and
mounted the train to Carlisle. Its cover contained the
grinning picture of a wimpy looking Jellyman clocking
on at the swimming pool. This torn treasure had been
salvaged from the waste paper bin and photocopied at
the central library.

Its deliberately obtuse banter would finally wind-up
in the staff common room of the council wags.

Question 1 Does the *Virgin* masturbate? If so, how
often?
Question 2 Does the *Virgin* only live with his
mother?
Question 3 Does his sister talk to the flowers?
Question 4 How old is the *Virgin*? A 6 B 14 C 33
Question 5 What are the *Virgin's* spare time
interests?

A Scuba diving
B Bungee jumping (from a Crane)
C Space Invaders

Question 6   Does the *Virgin* drink huge quantities of
beer to prove his manhood?
     Question 7   Can the *Virgin* phleg further than anyone
else?
     Question 8   Is the *Virgin* a clever and sophisticated
                  circumlocutor?
     Question 9   Does the *Virgin* tell tall stories?
     Question 10 *Prohibited!* Paid up member of 'Militant'?

*If you can answer the ten simple questions printed
above and identify the insidious character in the
photograph you could be on your way to winning a
fabulous star prize!*

All entries to be mailed direct to Mary Shithouse...

In the large bare waiting room a solitary heater pumped
out its paltry energy as a dim lit *Will O' the Wisp*
imposed a modicum of tinsel on the Alpine club.
     Through the surrounding smog *frogs and fishes* rilled
the railhead as she waited for the steamer to Larne.
     Suddenly a tall sturdy gentleman broke in from the
fell and shook his heavy mac against the radiator. He
trailed his ancient vintage *tourer* across the room to
stand against the plaster beside our hero's.
     The distinguished midnight passenger sat opposite
them and began pulling up his straps. He bent down to
examine the competition with an expression of lionize.
     The charismatic peer fingered the links of the
superior metal article with his coy prestidigitator and
verified they had been oiled sufficiently.
     Like a sublime weighing scale he patrolled the pair
of sleepy eyes with their mudguards incrustated from
coom. Sometimes wished he could be 'gathered.'
     "Going far?" he asked, picking sullenly at the
grime. Come to the mad-hatter's tea-party!
     He'd vanquished a few dragons in his time and had
entered the *hall of the slain.*

"You never know who you're going to meet on the Railway
line overnight. I know a lot of people who are just
too shy to strike up an acquaintance." He smiled
exposing a fine row of gleaming white huskers.

"Do either of you believe in second-sight?" asked
the figure-flinger. His large brown eyes were dilating
and he seemed to drift in closer. He wore a kilt with
nothing underneath.

"It depends what you mean by that," said the Flash,
always willing to enter a bite of logic-chopping.

A youth peered curiously over the top of his
benchmark as the stately *Rip Van Winkle* drew his
bulbous eyes and pondered for a moment.

"Do you believe in *re-incarnation!*" he cried. "Do
you believe in magic?" With his eye-teeth growing out
of focus he flew into a rage about Castles in the sky.

"I interpreted in their clarity a Rosetta Stone," he
inflected, beginning to pause in an ostentatious
manner.

Conraddin described his visitations to the overgrown
medieval churchyard where the locals all ran from his
manifestation. Clambering luminous among the hordes he
had eventually stumbled on his own heraldic trimming.

On the old abandoned slab he discovered the detailed
inscriptions consistent with his *genetic memory.* A so
called expert had been able to piece the puzzle
together and trace his tared family lineage to its
waist-line. A dead ringer?

"There was no other explanation possible," he
bellowed, gesticulating his long arms magnanimously
above his regal drive of snow; he was most certainly
descended from the Hohenstaufen Emperor; Conraddin 1!

At this point the artful and articulate pious fraud
reached a powerful bass crescendo of intensity.

Carmel began to giggle. Several explorers
pretending to read their guide books began to heave
with laughter. He bleated on wuthering heights.

Drew a dark line round everything. Black and white
aren't colours.

"But didn't he die at an early age; drowned in the sea
or something?" feigned the Flash.

Emperor Conraddin hovered for a second and then
interceded with various unexplained coincidences which
invited scepticism.

"I believe you, but thousands wouldn't," said F.
The youth made an imprint in wax. "Have you ever been
sectioned?"

The powerful spirit candidly studied the Flasher.
Perhaps he'd caught him making faces under the shade.
He lowered his gaze to the floor as the king shifted
towards the girl. Could hear a different drummer.

"I can always tell when someone is about to die,"
snuffed the Emperor. He shook his head grimly and
gloated behind his gauntlet.

"A year ago when a man from the village eloped with
my sweetheart..." he interceded. "I warned him he was
going on the great adventure in six months duration,
and he's not been the only one either!"

"What are you? Some kind of Banshee then?" asked F.
Emperor Conraddin tossed his thick white magne of
crinal locks and smirked so sovereignly at the balding
one. He zapped him out of existence!

The chattering piston of the glittering steel chaise
informed the jury as it lanced alongside the platform
kerb. It was a wise child that knew its own father.

"Don't get lost up in Glencoe will you?" smirked the
Emperor as he wheeled his bicycle up to the door.

"I've heard the weather can be very critical this
time of year." 'Over the hill, and on 'til Christmas.'

As he held the wooden lapel F. noticed how the
shouter had his arm wound around the responding woman.

He was already asking Carmel if she wanted to join
him on a cycling holiday along the Rhine next summer.
They were unfalteringly swopping items for future
reference as the loner retreated ignominiously...

Here was the night *male* crossing the border,
bringing the chink and the postal order...lurking
outside the shattered grill and charging down the

aisleways of the pigwagon. Even the heating was
banished in the cool of the Erebus.

F. awoke on the dismantled seat at seven o'clock
with early morning commuters clambering over his half
naked body lying across the gantry.

A crofter nearly fainted as the locomotive cascaded
through the golden moors and glens from Glasgow to
Ardlui. Where the engine slowed for a short expiry.

The familiar specter in an orange kagoole stared
searchingly through the laminated glass in the fog.

Flash ducked down in case the cyclist should
recognize him, and darted quickly behind the luggage
rack for a quick *strike*, looking for someone to blame.

It was a terrible season; the gale battled
unremitting throughout the whole period of his waiting.
A Stentorian hurricane blew incessantly along the
Queen's highway as if there was no tomorrow and pelted
its spume against the feeble human inhabitations.

Flashman sipped his third cup of coffee in the cafe
of Fort William, cupping his hands gently round the
fluid, and occasionally glancing at the large pair of
mammaries. White pride, worldwide!

Having recently exercised his categorical imperative
he still recalled that alleged accident with the
waterproofs caught on the cooker ring. Had he really
been so clumsy?

As the symphony played Vivaldi he admired himself
from a slightly different angle in the foyer perspex
and surveyed the harbour approach.

Where the sea raged like a tormented titan and flung
its gallons against the land, floating from the corner
of the vignette, he espyed an obscure figure tottering
into the district.

Tossed like a *drifter* the miserable leaf gradually
grew to more life like proportions during many minutes
of anxious wakefulness. Suddenly the biker leapt from
the image. He spun from the frame to see if it was not
only in his imagination. F. was always staggered by
the synchronicity of their wild conjunctions.

The saturated Jellyman soaked to the skin wearily dragged himself in and shivered round the soup.

"The devil damn thee black thou cream faced loon!" The Jellyman beamed with rapturous delight.

"All the way from the Capital in less than two days on a Mars bar and no leggings!" he tittered. "The last five miles against a headwind felt like felling a hundred. You're damned lucky to have a friend like me," he jibed. "Perhaps I'm not such a Jellyman afterall. Wish I was covered in soot."

"How are you?" he smiled. "Still saving yourself for someone special?"

The wet-faced youth suddenly reveilled with a fulsome pantomine of hydrophobia.

"Aren't you going to have a close shave?" he shuddered. "You look just like 'Captain Birdseye.' Still, I suppose we are both entering the 'twilight of our youth.'" A drowned rat!

He shuffled his feet under the diner and forced a self-conscious simper. J. riveted him that there were no such thing as mermen...

"You remind me of *Black Adder* with a tooth rising in the centre of his forehead," said F. "It's grown even bigger since the last time we met."

The true monarch of the mind felt the hump between his eyes (it was easy to imagine a horn sprouting from the bowl of his temple). He stamped his cloven foot and loosened the top of the tomato ketchup.

"I suppose we are pretty similar," he conceded. "Our life paths have both followed a consistently oblique orbit. But I still think you're wasting your opportunity. How will you ever learn to appreciate the complexities of existence in a fish-tank?"

"I've received some jolly good news!" twittered the Jellyman. "They're going away somewhere next weekend so *La Maison* will be free. You can sleep in my sister's spare bedroom."

Pity thought F.; he rather looked forward to the *aegis* of his mother's noisy snoring.

It was over the *last supper* that they first began
considering the bombardment of UNH with 16 Mev
deuterons through a 2-mil aluminium window.

The perennial scholar arriving unexpectedly had
nearly caught him peering through their peep hole...F.
sometimes referred to J. as the 'jerk who thought he
knew too many things.'

Waited on hand and foot the pair of wasters
conspired together on the outskirts of the canteen
while the primary hosts removed their plates and
brought fresh supplies blushing to their altar. The
Jellyman had the stomach of an Ostrich...

After partaking of orison the precocious *kelpy*
gathered round to test the tension in his biceps. The
warden's wife seemed worried in case they were too
bothersome. What he really needed was a volunteer
'taster.' Wait till you're drawing your pension!

"If you don't stop encouraging them we'll end up
being thrown out of here," slavered the Jellyman. "If
only I could enrol on another study course. My union
card has expired and I'll have to pay full fare soon."

"Where do you go to at night?" he asked. "I seem to
spend half my time trying to find out where you have
gone to. Look who left the door open..."

"You can certainly score with the chicks," he
squirmed..."I had another *bad dream* last night. A
dirty old Fisherman spurted pus all down my leg. Uugh!
That's the last time I'm stopping there!"

F. wouldn't tell him initially...'an emaciated
piglet had been grunting at the side of the track when
they picked him up in the tram and carried him inside.
After seven lean years the animal was returned to the
field fully ripened.'

"Ask the pig what his name is. You daren't tell
me!" tittered the Jellyman, focusing on his reluctance.

"What have you been doing? That teacher's certainly
got her eyes on you. I knew what you were the very
first second we met!" J. had a quiff like a ferret's
armpit but he made a good enough Fenian. He looked
just like a creature from the Serbonian bog.

"There's a *Cannibal* where I earn my bread. The women
are falling over themselves to feel the size of his
cock stretching their shaft. They say it's down to
personality but maybe the naked savages have metal in
their dreadlocks. The chief's are supposed to be able
to tie a knot in it! You never see one of them with a
lurcher. Whenever 'I' ask someone out they look the
other way. Do you think that all the *Milesian* bitches
are born *Molly Maguires?* Should we send them down
directly to Judge Thomas?"

"But we've been wearing woollens longer than they
have," sparked F. "Even as we speak they'll be parting
their prostrate canker. But the cunts are all the same
underneath their paint and varnish."

"I've done all I can to try and make them like me."
"Even to the extent of flowing round their rotten logs.
Yet I've still been left out in the cold. There ain't
no black in the Union Jack, so all you niggers fuck-off
back," he rasped.

"Ever since the afternoon my mother caught me
unawares I've lived my life in *suspended animation*; she
said I'd better stay away from the hen party. They say
the pattern of your existence is usually set by thirty
something so there's nothing I can do to prevent my
nascent *gene death*...though I'm glad she sucked the
poison from my snakebite."

Perhaps another smoke-screen? J. was always
blowing-off about something. He boasted that he'd had
a thousand buns in the oven.

"That's why you're the Jellyman!" laughed F. "I
always wondered why you never paid board. She gave you
a nice blow-job? 'Whom the Gods would destroy...'"

"*If truth were a woman,*" he jeered, and crunched his
pork scratchings. Jelly wiped his mouth on the back of
his sleeve as was his predilection. He held a smooth
pebble in his hand which had been baptised. Its
surface had been scuffed with 'Aunty Kay-horse' and he
plundered his left and right-sided awareness.

"Well I'm certainly not putting mine where the
primitive's had his," he fumed. "Although women can
make admirable friends that is not their *prime
function*. When did they last learn to communicate with
us? As mixed up as a blind lesbian in a fish market."

"*Out of Africa* they come, and other places too,
dragging their ponderous scrotum over jagged rocks and
fucking with the *crass Milesian* pin-up. It's bio-
chemical no doubt. She creams off the most desirable
mate to produce the fittest offspring. That is the law
and how it should be, spreading their foul disease.
But they've met their Water-loo. It came hurtling
through space and collided with our sunguard. Then a
particle shot straight up 'the Rock's bum. Hah! hah!
But it's only when they became birds of burden that
their cart became heavily bogged down in mud."

"So it's 'proof by potency' afterall," smiled F.
"The tree-dwellers Olympian image is one reason for
their success. Although they are certainly awarded
degrees on the basis of their roots and prepared the
manner to mumble. They probably have lower I.Q.'s on
the hole; but it's definitely the blood that thickens.
I suppose they gain strength from consuming all their
foes? And it's common knowledge that if one of their
young is born retarded they have their head bashed in
with a brick." A method for measuring 'pea' brains?

"We are the *dispossessed*; there are no insane. Our
embrace with world are the wounds that make us wise."

"We will eventually enter into the kingdom of the
deep with the aid of our cradle song. Dirty tricks
will always triumph over the common weal."

"And the condusive psychologist who believes he
knows our raison d'etre. Once the appearance falters
then ruthless nature thumbs the ground."

"Teach them to miter with *Black Gladiators*. And
harrassment is only in 'their' skin."

"If they did become the Guardians it really would
become the 'Planet of the Apes.' But he'll soon turn
her into an old gimmer. Aye, the bigger they are the
quicker they go out of fashion."
     "Yet it is from their low ranks novel flowers must
bloom? A black ram tupping our white ewe...that's
totally democratic! Just try sending him through the
pass for his oats and he'll crown it by claiming *unfair
dismissal*. I've a good mind to start a local chapter
of the 'Klu Klux Klan.' A 'Fad,'" he cried. "That's
it! Fucking Anthropophagists. I wish they'd eat their
nuts! In the race to fertilize her eggs she believes
his every word. Is variety the spice of life afterall?
I have observed the bare knuckles of the lower
primates."
     "How deep does the English Rose really grow? Her
roots are not even shallow!"
     "You will get a stalk-on when 'I' command," orders
the *Milesian* crone. "Nobody decrees when to spill my
seed and I'm not sliding in on his fetid spunk! It's
nothing more than 'One-upmanship. That's scandalous!
And they say there's plenty more living-space for the
billion or so on the way."
     "Anyway I'm glad you're not into ethicalcleansing!"
Peering through the glass darkly.
     "I was only testing you. Say, how do you get a part
on 'After Dark?'" he flipped..."Whip a Cannibal and
have Mrs. T. for breakfast. I drouth for a face of
sloe. They can even lick their own genitals."
     "An eye for an eye, a tooth for a tooth," he hissed.
"I'm a flower of the flock as well! Let the rabble
sell their pots and pans in the poxy market place but
never let them champion *sexual fascism*."
     "What's the lowest form of life then?" asked F.
"A Pimp?" answered the *enigmatic* Jellyman slithering
over the bilge as they called the crack of doom.
     "A Hypocrite!" said the Flashman. "So why don't you
get a flipping move on?"

"Mind your own funny business!" scowled the Jellyman
like a latent flash of lightning.

His soggy lips turned dry and his symbols crashed
from the stratosphere.

"Well, how's the treatment coming along?" asked F.
He tried to steer clear of dangerous waters.

The old ally was undergoing hypnosis for his
perspiration.

J. reckoned to jerk his head as if he were tony.
On the outside there appeared a witty and skilful
circumlocutor, but in the interior a little green worm
gnawed subtly at his unstable cerebral cortex.

Trying to pin him down was like attempting to tie
the Bishop of Durham to a definite article of faith,
and at any moment he could suddenly *riot* resulting in
the inevitable schism.

From the Hostel in the sump they cycled up the
gathering gradient past the Highland Bull and entered
through the vermicular wynd to the topmost crag linked
by protoplasm to the arching ring of the ecliptic.

The sun was still shining faithfully and flushed the
peaks with candour. A golden Eagle sculled high above
the vanquished seamen duelling in the lower meadow...

Caught in the mare's tail their intention was to
guzzle for a while on the dirge of the mighty McDonald
before flitting across the bleak plateau of Rannock
Moor, and then freewheeling down the *black python* to
Crianlarich.

Underhill the 'Overmen' perched on the precipice
like a Griffin and the Chimera prepared to continue
their amaranthine of expletive deletives.

With cautious scepticism they affirmed the 'New Age'
of Oberon and the re-awakening of their natural
dynamism. It gave added punch to Doyle's expression
'the coming of the Fairies.' On a clear day from the
Empire of the Sun one was able to sweep over four
different land masses.

"A debate should be drawn like a circle and always
finish where you started. It's all a question of
ergonomics."

"Last night I dreamt that I turned into a brown
paper bag and blew all the way to the Moon!"

He returned to the awkward subject of their
catalogue.

"When the last band of Nature Spirits were leaving
the islands their holy prince repined that not even the
most secret havens were safe."

Have you ever noticed the shape of Toadstools?
Jellyman repeated that devouring power plants made him
feel a hundred foot tall. He spoke in a weird dialect.
Was it the J. or something more sinister?

"I never spoke a word until I reached puberty at
ten," he digressed. "Everyone thought that I was a
dumb oaf. They wanted to send me to a 'special
school,' but my mother interceded. I was petrified of
people at that age. Even my sisters ran away and
called me names. At school they used to call me
'Slider;' I was six foot tall at fourteen when I broke
the hall mirror. I wouldn't give them the steam off
my..."

"But now I'm the 'Lord of Reflections,' he cackled.
"Wait till I get back! Even the Janitor was afraid.
But the worse thing I ever did was read all those
pseudo-intellectual books," he protested. "I think
it's all a wild goose chase. If Mankind was on fire I
wouldn't even piss on the flames. I hate our fucking
sun!" Shaking his fist in defiance.

"If only there was some way that I could prevent my
shuck from decaying. I might smash this boulder down
on top of that lambs' skull, but would I become the
ruler of all that. Don't you realize what's been
happening? All those brazen manifestations are a
result of your early religious gangrene. I wish that
you could exorcise your past the way that I exercise my
tongue. Wouldn't you rather drive a stake into the
molten core of Adam."

F. began to deny the gem of his idea. But the truth
was beginning to emerge and he had to keel the wizard.

"Tradition has it that there were three trolls
snoozing in a lair," said F. "One of them suddenly
said to the other two..."Do you want to hear a
story?...There were three dragons lying in a den
playing backgammon, when the eldest of them roared to
those remaining..."Do you want to hear a plot?...There
were three trolls snoozing in a lair..." So he recited
the legend anyhow; it was a *Ripping Yarn*! There was no
sitting on the fence this time.

"Uugh! That's revolting!" hissed the knave. He
frowned at him with utter repugnance. "Didn't anyone
ever find out? I wonder how Havelock Ellis would have
argued for sexual static." He cogitated for a while.
"But Stephenson had the 'Brownies' to help him, or was
it the Girl Guides?" he giggled.

"Still, you can't fool the people all of the time."
"When I was a little boy my mother said that I would
lose my magic powers if I ever lost my purity. That
the strongest ram grew the densest fleece."

Jelly looked askance; he was undoubtedly an
unnatural socialist underneath and tried to avoid the
ensuing subject. "What about the age of consent then?"
he added. "With what would you then re-place it?
Would there be any upper limit?"

"The lottery of law. Perhaps there really are 'rats
among the cornfields.' Spawned by the ten spurious
oaths. Didn't Ovid once say that 'Human interference
has imposed spiteful laws, so that jealous regulations
forbid what nature itself allows!' As I think we've
said before; 'the elemental is always the most vital.'
But it's really just a lot of fuss about nothing."

"*Heroes and Villains*. Real or just imagined. It's
a statistical fact that a vestal virgin falling
pregnant for the very first time usually gives birth to
a healthy infant unless preveniently terminated."

"True love with her Svengali can result in him feasting
on the Queen's squalid heap for a lifetime (J. fidgeted
and pretended he had not heard that fatal word 'love').
The cloner can bugger his lad until all hell freezes
over but that's all tidy and legal. I prefer to use a
wheelbarrow for pushing it myself! *Uranus* was created
for shitting down was it not? Though they could
perhaps stem the rising tribalism."

"So far as I'm aware it was designed for no other
purpose. Did you know what the *Franciscan Frier* was
rumoured to do to his cattle? Now, that's what you
call *crossfertilization!* I don't suppose anyone can
help their *sexual preference*," he altered.

"What does A.I.D.S. stand for?...Arse injected death
syndrome!" he sniggered. "When have you ever seen two
rodents at it?"

"But surely some of them are not mentally mature
enough. Isn't that often the common objection?" He
pointed along the ley to the Saracen brick.

"I lay claim to the air particles in my fist! I've
met women in their twenties without their house in
order. How do you define mental maturity. By the
ritual drinking of latex? If they do it too is that a
perversion?" The Angel's war→··

"Do you really desire to be on the side of angels?
Why don't you put an advert in the local mag; 'Paedo
Babysitting Services!' and see what response you get.
Entreat Amnesty International to make a declaration on
your behalf," he chuckled, swallowing the penultimate
dregs of his Tartan mead. "Sixteen thousand billion
black birds baked in a PIE!"

"What's good enough for John Lackland is good enough
for me. Their kisses are as light as those May-flies
which graze the great transparent lakes at sunset. We
have a commendable group of supporters already,
although because life is so unworthy of ⌣ye they are
not always so explicit in their taciturn depravity.
Everyone's heard of the American King for instance; the

fabled piano player; our film director friend to name
but a few, and have you seen the current listing of the
'Flander's Mare.' But I really think it was Pope Borgia
who sullied the name of sexual deviancy from the
poisoned chalice of the clergy. That which a present
age considers to be evil is usually just a welcome
rumble of what a future epoch will deem to be an
auspicious windfall. I admired his sense of
determination."

"We're not talking now about the precocious *little
people* who start their periods at eleven or so. Our
ultimatum is the *last taboo*...Everybody knows that
physical maturity is a bar to lifelong membership.
Have you ever noticed the complete absence of pubic
hair among the *Tuatha* for instance, and does it really
matter how right-minded they are? There'll be no more
messy backstreet abortions in our lifetime."

"We will call ourselves the *Children of the elder
statesman* and *our* ambrosia will be the fruit of their
honey. Remember that their bud is softer than the
thawing flood and their marrow never wanes. Although
the big bang always comes in the form of great untold
destruction I would certainly make apostles of the
Daanites. The meek *shall* inherit the earth! There's
real importance in being earnest."

"But how will you do this?"
"I will do this through the skald's *five pointed star.*
The letters are my building blocks and the spaces my
roof timber. When you make the two one, and when you
make the inner as the outer, and the outer as the
inner, then shall you enter the kingdom...To write the
liturgy in Gaelic so the mass can't recognize. We
wonder lost throughout the Universe and surrender to
our fate."

"The sweetest Circe who tempts you ever on-wards.
We will not give them up! We will not give them up to
lies at all! And *we are not in need of any balm on
troubled waters.* A hex on pathetic pity. Our elixir

will be their worship of the magnificence. We can lead
them to the lost Continent *under the tender
archipelago*. Now 'that's' *Utopia!* I'd call it. But
when you spy a lusty infant make sure it's not just a
pigmy standing favourably on the horizon."
     "I bet I could abuse nine in one swimming session!"
"But a people ruled by winds and whirlpools cannot ever
be taken to the cleaners. All you'll need is a musical
pipe to lead them down into the cavern...although I've
heard it's best to bugger them initially. There's
nothing else to quell the current tide of *tort* than to
bring back *child prostitution* for the Father's sake.
Or start a concubine of them."
     "Yes! That's it entirely," said the Flash. He fell
upon his words. 'But if romantic *love is dead* long
live the *minotaur!*'
     "Have you noticed how a *cult* is usually
characterised by a fearless leader who claims divinity
or a special mission delegated to him by a supreme
being? Though we're bound to encounter opposition from
the establishment we will not go down without a
castrametation." Take me to the...
     "Why don't you just let sleeping dogs lie?"
The black cloud gathering round the summit of Ben Nevis
looked daggers over the moor. A viperous blizzard
tumbled over the heather and a pig in a poke entered
his frame of mind. The yellow streak running down
Jelly's transexual vertebrae trickled with urine once
more. But he still managed to fish-out a pre-meditated
wrangle although he must have felt almost on the verge
of throwing himself over the brink.
     "But what is truth? You can't even prove your own
physical presence. Have you ever sought help for
this?" he enquired..."I know, you carry the sack, and
I'll push them in..."
     "No fear! I like to trap them by myself."
"That's the biggest load of rhubarb I've ever heard. I
wish you'd just put a lid on it. Did you know that

punishment started as a pit at the bottom of the cliff
to dump your Dr. Fell! Fight fear with the devouring
element."

He shot the snot out of his nose with the sneak of
his left hand; a new trick which he had copied from
some of the kids at the coop. With his finger in the
breeze he tested the direction of the chinook.

"As sure as the orb rises in the east at daybreak
you'll end up being sent to the city Penitentiary by
the translators and robbed of all that is most
enjoyable in your existence. I hope no-one goes around
accusing me of being normal," hissed J.

"It's not that I disagree with you," he said. "But
do you really want a raw-head to take advantage of a
sweet and vulnerable young child?"

They stared skyward and pondered the
transmogrification in the heavens.

"They kill martyrs like harts. Completely lacking
support the *hoi polloi* will brand you an 'object
detester' and will tear you into *disassociate* units.
They might even bring back hanging just for you,
although that will not prolong your misery into
positive discrimination. They'll scatter all your
ashes and pour scorn on all your arguments. I wouldn't
be surprised if you earned the nickname of the 'Mabus!'
And you will have to act quite naturally according to
your label. What if they're right," he shivered.
"What if there are such creatures as Friar Rush. I
would rather you gave me a toothpick to jump into the
wolf pit..."

"That's Balder-dash! It occurs in every ward of
creation. If we cause them to think again then that
too is totally admirable. Their Talmud is written by
'men' to be broken by 'men' also. Is that too a crime?
Whose law is it anyway? We are simply unaccustomed to
this hybrid iconography in the eugenical void. How
could we remove a worm from the woodwork? Steel is
tempered in the furnace."

"There's nothing debase about subduing or having the

will to dominate. Why shouldn't they receive a liberal
education? We pay libations to this *tainted love* with
the sparks of our own awareness. Madness is what the
rabble calls light shining from another place. There
comes a time when every child must leave its earthly
parents, and who knows, there may still be fledgling
planets to conquer."
    "*Excellent feast!*" cackled the Jellyman
palingenesis.
    He was just rising to celebrate the founding of a
their new world order by brandishing the 'ramus' at the
bird of ill omen when he was splashed by the gliding
eaglet from above.
    "The younger the better! How soon before you can
fix me up with a gaggle? 7's always been my lucky
number!" he cried.   "For theirs is the kingdom the
power and the glory, for ever and ever, Amen." he sang.
"Absolutely no necessity to wear a condom," he chuckled
with glee. "Here's looking at ya kid!"
    "Too long in the tooth," said F. "I prefer them
when they first come out of the kiln and are still hot
and slippery."
    "Tell me the meaning of the Outlaws?" hissed
Bogarte nos na goithe.
    "To extinguish 'old life forms,' and bring forth the
Admirable Crichton!"

As the lone cyclist approached Chesterfield's crooked
spire F. chatted up the actress on the intercity
streaking in the opposite direction.
   The flaxen-haired Geraldine said that she was
rehearsing 'Romeo and Juliet' at the Crucible.
   "It's my favourite role," she frankly admitted.
"Although I've played the part many times before, I do
hope that everything goes well on the night of our
opening performance."
   F. quoted his remarkable repertoire of lines,
finishing with the words; "But soft, what light through
yonder window breaks, it is the east and Juliette is
the sun..." Looked as if he'd turned over a new leaf.
   She clapped and sounded most impressed. "I think
you must know the scenes better than I do," she teased.
"Are you some kind of griffonage?"
   "This and that!" snapped the Flash, undoing his
flies ready for action. "But mostly 'that,'" he
muttered drearily, intent on offering her membership of
the famous 125 club. They had their 'Rushdie.'
   "Do you read Brecht," she asked. "I'm not a
literature scholar myself, but I've heard he's fairly
substantial." F. threw a damper on it.
   "I prefer Ibsen," disclosed the Flash. But it was
hard to concentrate hiding a nice stiff thyrsi beneath
the copy of Faust. A fine display of Caber-tossing.
   Unfortunately she had noticed his Tarot cards. He
realized that he was not going to get any peace until
she'd had her fortune done...What was so special about
a 'Tall dark stranger' anyway?
   "Fancy a drop of spirit?" she gleaned. Geraldine
was suprisingly coy to say she spent so much of her
occupation warbling under the dramatic nimbus.
   "We're going to see Amadeus this evening," she
smiled. "Next week we are attending the last night at
the proms! So glad you asked."
   What new 'stations of the Cross' would we have to
erect?

Meanwhile the bleater was once more phoning his ma-ma.
"Hello, it's only me!" he said. "Has anybody rang yet?
I've been waiting hours for him," he whimpered. "This
is the final straw. I'm not going to be messed around
any longer." Could hardly run between two lamp-posts.

He pushed his way through the crowd of the packed
auditorium and prepared to start the swim without his
missing adjutant...it was definitely who you knew.

"Last weekend I was the cockswaine in a ladies
regatta," mustered Geraldine. But there was a *Black
Swan* look about her. Could she have been a *secret
agent*? We are creatures of the Flash!

He crossed his legs away from her solicitude with
absolute clarity. Although F. had already missed his
stop twice and had been acting rather outlandish to put
it mildly, she still helped him to the egress with his
bicycle, and carried his holdall for him past the
ticket snout. Hath he the power to procreate?

"Do you always expose yourself to girls you meet on
the train?" she winked. "I do hope you decide to
write..." There but for the disgusting grace of God.

On the beach of the ice-capped silver thaw where the
Triathlon was being held the competitors were already
concluding a crawl twice around the atoll. Their next
stage was a thirty-five mile cycle ride, and then they
culminated with a full marathon.

A daymare shroud shuttled over the trees as the
Jellyman approached the edge of the water like a pipe
cleaner's Captain Webb...always gonna be winners.

J. shivered hideously as he dipped his toe in the
ice-box. "It's cold as a frog!" screeched a chap,
returning to have a towel thrown around him by his
loving spouse...trunks made by 'E-di-puss.'

With iron-grit determination writ across his brow
the fundamental womanly leapt bravely into the fog
bank, and landed belly-flop in the drink, just inches
in depth at that ebb on the sand. Donkey!

Dragging himself along the pebble strewn bottom the
Jellyman waded unobstructed into the unlucky mist
determined to get on with his dowsing. It shat from a
great height...could it have been an aeroplane?

~~With goose-pimples loaded on his white mystified body~~
he swam once around the route just to keep his
vellicating maulstick from suffering frost bite.

When the Flash at last made it to the event a large
group of onlookers were gathered around the water's
edge. The St. John's Ambulance were placing something
on a stretcher from the deep chilling depths.

The white chloroformed body of a *Jellyfish* was
loaded on board as he called out despairingly from the
van. Freedom of speech conformed to the Norm. Had his
head blown clean off. The 'man of steel.' Think
devil. Flies on the same piece of shite.

"Where've you been all this time?" he pandered
faintly. "Why does the fish-plate take longer than my
bicycle to arrive at any given destination?"

"Maybe it's time for a change," he tendered. "It's
only because of you *infecting* me with your evil star
that I'm in this rotten predicament. Well, say
something, even if it's goodbye."

"I know," said F. "But never let it be said that I
knew! One day all will be revealed. Loving their
childlike follies their lies belie their frailty."
[This new constellation; the 'Toad' named after him.]

"It's been scientifically proven! Only the good die
young."

"Any mention of this and you'll be out on your ear!"

If he'd worn a suit of lead it would have been easier
to see through his metal.

"You have a woman's cunning. If you'd been born with a
red nose I'd have called you a prize bitch!"

Something totally uncivilized about civilized society.
The persecution of rival factions.
"I don't want to know your reasons. Just shut the fuck
up!"

Even the gods are cut down to size.
'I'd rather be an Arthur than a don Quixote!'

X

LABURNUM WOOD

The Black widow removed her finger suggestively from her lip and belvedered his trump. Who on earth could have sent him a UB40? He wasn't seriously contemplating his golden handshake just yet.

"Not much luck there love," she smiled. "Perhaps another shuffle of the deck will bring you what you're looking for. Your fortune seems to indicate entire seclusion from the general public at least until the prentice phase."

"I'm so glad we've stumbled on each other," she shone... "and just around the corner. I'm a little guarded towards men since my early childhood experiences as you can imagine, but you seem harmless enough, although you tell me you're still single?"

"According to your palm a vindictive woman means to do you harm...but remember that life is really what you make it."

"A holiday you say. Which part of the Black country?"

Just as he was about to plight his trust in her Bernice signalled the epilogue of the betting shop. The clockwork man jerked solemnly to her rear effluence. Four hours in her *boudoir* made a nice change from the oft deserted bridewell.

"Drop by any time," she laughed. The *Sibyl* gently closed the door after him and rang her dearest *Sappho* as quick as a lamplighter. Lending another string to the bow.

"Yes, a complete loner," she scathed. "I wouldn't be surprised if he committed hara-ki-ri one day..."

F. emerged from the station at Slippery Ford to riddle the rebus which led to 'Little Ranger.'

Although the circus was notoriously difficult to discover he was directed by the dragoman over the *turnstiles.*

After checking in with the warden the jinx parked his
bicycle and motored stiffly into the meeting room where
his associate supined relaxedly by the fire.

The Jellyman had undergone a radical
transformation...

He now sported a full Mediterranean sun-tan and his
jeans were designer label. The holes in his shoes had
vanished, and even his fingernails had been clipped!

Gone too were the tinted spectacles which had been
disguising the Mariner's piercers. To aid him with his
myopia were an expensive pair of contact lenses.

His daily routine was speaking volumes in a rapid
toning of his sinews.

His cool dark floss was glamorously flicked back,
and coralled with the latest hair gel for the
dude...he'd even had a blonde streak dyed.

Even the *Crow's nest* which had been forming round
his eyes had been miraculously ironed-out. The chicks
no longer called him a beach-ball. Had he been
drinking from the magic cauldron? He felt like a new
man. Had become an expert in 'women's studies.'

When J. had fortunately collided with a truck he had
limped his way to a jackpot..!

As the shoal of Hibernian long-hairs cooked their broth
he introduced the warp-twister with 'I've discovered
Shangri-La!'

"Someone let the cat out of the bag," he glared..
"But it'll take more than that to elicit my nigger in
the woodpile."

The squeeling squadron situated around him quietly
huddled closer and one by one fled to the other side of
the cabin...

"Looks like the *Fat Controller*!" giggled Alison.
"The *kiss of death!*" tittered the Jellyman, raddled by
his embarrassment. "I never know what you're going to
say next," he hissed.

"They've seen your *evil eye*. You haven't lost your
touch then? When can you go in for another hair
transplant...there are still some gaps in your scalp."

"Shouldn't it be booked during your next free period?
Nobody I know looks like you," whimpered the *moaning
Minnie*. "I think that we are heading inevitably for
opposite sides of the Pole."

  "I was wrong to take so little care of my
appearance," he smiled. "People take so much for
granted on first impressions. It's all about keen
marketing," he grinned. "You have to learn the soft
cell. Just continue to look on the bright side and
never say anything too controversial. Sticking above-
board lands you in the dog-kennel."

  "No-body can pull the birds like I can!" He even
said that he had never been blown-out in his life.

  "Jenny has invited me down to the pub for a while,"
he flowed. "You can come along if you like. If you
behave yourself. Would you like to lend my hair gel?
Always take the fair elements with you," he bleated.

  While the charabanc trecked down the Patagonian
heights and into the black abyss F. singled one out
from the herd and began by making advances...after
helping her over the fence in his arms she suddenly
darted along the trail and caught the others.

  "Rape!" she screamed as F. appeared from the
insubstantial blotter holding up his limbs.

  "Is your friend a *Bodybuilder?*" asked the Scottish
Lion. Like shit to a shovel...

  "If he walked through a stone wall would he leave
his shape outlined in the bricks? He's got arms like
blooming treetrunks."

  "He's never taken steroids, that I know of," shifted
K.Y.J...

  "I hope you are all taking note of the lie of the
land?" said F. But no-one seemed to be listening to
him gossiping in the basin.

  The tribe found a cosey space in the local tavern
while F. cranked self-consciously to the bar...Jelly
settled down to manna in the wilderness.

  His increased responsibilities were giving him extra
confidence and he now projected a felicitous persona.

In the vaporous tap-room F. felt positively caustic.
His arm-pits displayed remarkable signs of fluid
retention.

He cavorted under the harsh beam of the Argand with
the bridge of his bonce gleaming like an airport runway
attacked with *cluster bombs*. Tick as a plank. The
family likeness was amazing, beggorah!

"Dearie me, just look at your friend," sniffed the
squatter as they nudged each other crossly and pulled
rude faces.

"Which planet has he come from? I bet it's just to
grab the headlines. Does he always move his neck like
that or is it musclebound? I thought he was your
museum piece when he arrived in the cabin...I'm very
sceptical about these macho types. My own estimation
is that they are extremely insecure individuals who
lack assurance of their manhood."

"What happened to him?" said one. "Has he had an
illness, or has he always been like that?" asked
another. She said a nice drop of amyl nitrate would
help him un-wind.

Why couldn't he form an orderly queue with his
replies? It was nice of you to ask.

F. flexed his biceps and rotated his head sideways.
"Mine's a large one!"

"That's not what I heard," quipped Fanny.
"Is anyone sat-ere?" J. sniggered.

. For the very first time the Jellyman suddenly wanted
to buy his own round and insisted on moving next to
Judy.

"You ought to have heard some of the things they
have been saying about you while you were away," he
whimpered. He scowled when he thought they were not
looking.

"If you don't ring the changes she'll be calling for
the Feds. It only takes a postcard to your bosses."

"Even the *fatgirl*?" sighed F. with alarm.
"Especially that packet of lard!" snickered the
Jellyman turning red. "They think you're crazy as a
Kinnock!" he wobbled.

J. had more skin changes than an itchy chamelion.

"I'm sick of having to apologise for your appearance," he added. "Why don't you just wear a wig. It'll keep your head warm in winter. You'll be ostracized permanently if you don't start adapting yourself. All my other friends are six-foot four professionals!" he wittered.

Jelly suddenly mutated a Homeric titter. He said that he had no intention of seeking out the limelight for himself.

"But you can't *appease* the plebs in perpetuity," groaned F. Controller.

"You've come down in the world since our days at college, sssh! they're talking!" - J.

Once more the isochronous mob erupted into a R-O-A-R of applause for their bearded savant's leading strings.

Every commonplace note *Vadar* uttered was greeted with outstanding gas as if he was the very *Apollo of the clowns.*

"Fancy a game of skittles?" The Jellyman was the first to be picked to partner Janine. Her father was a stockbroker. As if that's important.

Downing his Dutch courage with increased speed the leper was deserted in the nook tapping his foot like a March Hare, and sending out bad vibes by the handful in all directions. Gave everyone the creeps.

"Your turn," they said, but you could tell they didn't really want him there. The Flasher was making even the definitive leader awkward, and he was also too cramped to throw.

After the game the coterie returned to the fiery little centre where the maniac stared with apprehension at their approach.

He tried to begin a conversation, but *Darth Vadar* steeped his thunder.

Once more the edges of the fringe echoed with the flippers of clapping seals...

"Did you understand the meaning of that joke?" he asked. The Jellyman began to flap with delayed reflex...

"What do you do for a living?" asked the girls. "Are
you a male model."
    "I'm a badminton coach!" snapped the Jellyman
blithely..."Oh, him...I believe he's a...Singleman?"
swivelling on his seat. "You'll have to ask him for
yourself. I don't know anything about it...perhaps
he's just a Jellyman."
    "Actually, I'm an *itinerant pyrotechnologist!*"
blushed F. They perlustrated blankly at him...and
yawned. J. had no strongly held convictions.
    But it soon came around to the traditional time for
knocking the Iron lady...even as the evening was
thawing to a close.
    Jelly was right on cue.
"Those bloody Tories!" he lamented. "Thatcher's
Britain! They're all a toffy nosed bag of lousy
'gits.' Why don't they just load them all in the dog
van and take them down to the river, after skinning
them alive and making leather handbags from their
callous crust. At least that way they could be put to
some good use! Send the press into quarantine."
    The general idea seemed to go down well, and he was
rewarded with a fraternal pat on his uliginous back as
he looked round smiling all the time. And it was quite
permissable to use subliminal brain-washing.
    "It's the old cow's birthday today," bleated the
girl with Amazonian zeal. "What do you think we should
buy her?"
    "A ticket to Mars?" ejaculated the Jellyman
immediately responding to her prompt.
    "How about the Welsh windbag's roasted head on a
platter with an apple to cork its mouth'?" sparked the
Flash. Had a Snowman suddenly entered the spot and
left the door open? "Er, well, they all 'piss in the
same pot anyway'..." he vacated.
    J. said that if the GREAT DOME were to be overturned
it could hold 3½ billion pints!

The midnight wanderers stepped into the great unknown.
Darth Vadar led the route, but didn't seem to know
where he was damn well going...F. wasn't sure if the
woods were a safe place to loiter.

The Highland lassie who had been so morose in F.'s
company automatically linked up with the malignant
Jellyman as if they'd known each other for years,
flirting and revealing the intimate details of her
tender moments. Bashing the bishop.

F. tried to tell a joke. 'What did the Catholic
bishop of Belfast say when the Protestant bishop of
Belfast died? - 'He's about to find out who the real
bishop of Belfast is.' But it fell on deaf ears.

J. flattered her with his most recent 'Pop star
hype' and laughed facetiously whenever it was expected.
The loyal and trusted Judas goat had an Albatross tied
around his neck. Signpost to 'Toot-an-car-moon!'

"One of them was so big he almost split me in half!"
she shuddered, and whispered something lewdly in his
ear...sewer rabbits scurried along before.

The timeless ones stooped into the bottomless
vacuum. They were led tripping through the contours on
the weird vortex of their quest by the hirsute
Confucius, to the Charybdis of the wheel's spinning
bramble. A ship of wooden 'Sleepers.'

The harvest crescent had been burgled. On and on
forever the notorious jungle of the Jet black wood
gradually annihilated their inebriety.

F. followed on behind bruising his carefully
lacquered armadillo against a passing larch.

J. was spinning his well-rehearsed seine of hanky-
panky. Called 'him' the 'laird of dirty dreams.'

"Let's push-off from that creep and sneak away by
ourselves somewhere under the roof!" Just loud enough
for him to discriminate in the dead centre of the wood.

She diminished into the secure pectoral of J.'s
shoulder. Scrape it off her shoe. Working-out.

Though Jelly's legs were rickety thin, she seemed
intent to praise them..."What I need is a real man,"
crooned the Jezebel idolizing up at him.

"Don't look at me," whimpered the Jellyman in his
high pitched wail. "I'm just a poor dumb male."

"He's not a man, he's a minx," muttered the
malcontent. He was determined not to let them out of
his sight and felt as if he were treading water.

The spineless one was investing his standard bearer
~~about the multi-nationals being responsible~~ for all the
corruption in the world when suddenly he fell over and
out popped his contacts into the black gloom at his
feet...if you can't do the time don't do the crime!

"How old are you?" asked the woman sticking to his
side. F. hadn't a cat in hells' chance.

"How old do I look?" he tittered childishly.
"Oh, about nineteen!" she guessed.

J. did not reveal why his sister called him the
'little boy who never grew up!'

"You look great!" gasped the girl. "How do you
manage to look so young?"

The Jellyman hiccuped..."I eat *blackbird's foetus's
on the eve of every full moon'*," he bragged...the girl
reacted with absolute enamour. He was obviously still
suffering from 'Munchhausen's disease!'

Jenny asked to go and see a 'man about a dog' while
the Jellyman held her hand in case she tripped and
'lost her balance.' Pair of fire-flies.

Four hours more had still not brought them any nearer
to base so *Worzel Gummidge* decided to climb to the top
of the rotting hulk of an Ash stripped of its bark to
see if he could see anything above the treeline. They
jostled to know Jelly's opinion.

"Where are all the natives?" cried Jack. "Let's
have a pewage and scoff its vital organs."

He shinnied back down the trunk to the earthy crew
at the root and picked up *Lia Fail* lying on the frond.

"Sandbag the scavenger!" howled the protege foaming
at his mouth. "Devour the Jackal before the flock of
Condors get him!"

When it emerged that Vadar had been gay all along J.
decided to make himself scarce...

With the first rays of Ariel's scarlet dawn the
hoods of the wood synchronized against the skyline like
a black charcoaled moke.

Then someone asked. "Where's Jenny gone?"
The screech of flint crashed like a starburst into the
globe...a hissing of potent firecracker...sputniked by
a treble squawk.

Along the promontory of land *Darth Vadar* charged with
his merry band of *Merpersons*, until they approached a
charcoloured clearing where Jenny stood there dabbing
her eyes as the sparks flew upwards.

She tugged on Vadar's rich bronze sleeve hardly able
to take sustenance. Mother Nature. Elf-shot!!

On the steaming patch of soil a whiff of Peppermint
permeated the ether ethnically cleansed at that very
same spot where they planted their crops.

In the first instance they assumed the incident to
be a clear case of *Spontaneous Humane Combustion*, but
the wisest of them knew the kelson number.

On the crutch of Gae's clouts, beneath a tiny wisp
of smoke, Nigel Bates sprawled forever phantasm...his
tongue had been throttled, his temperament skinned
alive. There was a gnashing of virulent tongs.

The remnants of his synged limbs rested loosely by
his silent trunk. You had to admire his Gadarine
swine.

F. was over the moon...Upon his temple and
remarkably untouched was a large pair of black framed
spectacles!

Biography

Born on Groundhog Day 1956, son of an English schoolteacher and regularly battered by a semi-literate Irish labourer, with a reading age of nine, and member of Sinn Fein. Was brainwashed at a local Catholic Grammar school but was expelled for setting light to the headmaster's study and refusing to get their hair cut. Suffered from socio-phobia while still living among humanity but continued to be kind to animals. Studied Astrology and the black arts but never became totally insane until meeting their former childhood sweetheart in 1999.

- ✓ Expounder of nightmares
- ✓ Slanderer of medical practitioners
- ✓ Former Belly-button Fluffer
- ✓ Expert in counter intelligence (able to track down any individual across the entire planet)
- ✓ Can see into the future and predict what is going to happen with the use of a tripod and the assistance of a third eye

---

BANNED FROM UNIVERSITY PRECINCTS, CHURCHES AND LIBRARY SPACES THROUGHOUT THE COUNTRY

Other books in which the Author had some in-put:

Widening Underground, Criminal Tendencies, Offensive Behaviour, Alien Intelligence, Odd bent Coppers, Natural Surveillance, Trades of the Toadman, **Dance of the red-crowned Prince.**

Hrothgar's lost parchments (not to be confused with 'Lost Parchments of the Arian Friars').

9 781978 259058